Praise for *Dignity & Justice*

"*Dignity & Justice* is a remarkable testament to the enduring values of spiritual solidarity and legal justice when faced with the agonizing predicament of unaccompanied children who, in crossing the southern border of the United States, face a life-or-death predicament. If they are refused asylum, they have to return to the brutal conditions from which they ran for their lives; if they are welcomed in the spirit of strangers respected for their human rights, they will grow up to believe in the equitable and emancipatory ideals of citizenship. Which side are you on? After reading Linda Dakin-Grimm's splendid narrative of the struggle of bereft families and the courage and hope of their children, there is only one side to be on—and it is the side that is both ethically right and politically just. Read on . . ."

—Homi K. Bhabha
Anne F. Rothenberg Professor of the Humanities
Harvard University

"*Dignity & Justice* considers Christ's simple, inexorable command: to love one another as he loved us. Dakin-Grimm brings the 'issue' of immigration alive with the stories of warm, breathing human beings who, like us, have dreams for our children; who, like us, long to make the world a better place; and who, unlike most of us, are fleeing intolerable danger and corruption in their countries of origin. She breaks down the labyrinthine, Byzantine immigration laws so that a layperson can at the very least understand the almost insurmountable obstacles faced by those who try to enter the United States. She sets forth the clear, unequivocal Church teaching on our obligation to welcome the poor, the war-torn, and the alien. She poses the question we will all face one day: Not whom did you vote for? Not where did you stand on any given 'political' matter? Rather, with Christ's eyes bearing down on ours: How did you treat the least of these?"

— Heather King, author of *Shirt of Flame:*
A Year with St. Thérèse of Lisieux

"The treatment of children at the southern border has become a focal point of America's often contentious debate on immigration. In *Dignity & Justice*, many of these children have confided in Linda Dakin-Grimm their darkest moments, from stories of gang persecution, to accounts of abandonment and domestic abuse, while she helps them navigate a Byzantine legal system that can grant them protection but also send them back to the places from which they fled. Over the years, the U.S. government has mostly sought to discourage these minors from journeying north, instituting policies of deterrence that have become increasingly more stringent under the Trump administration. In this intimate, yet nuanced chronicle, Dakin-Grimm argues for a more egalitarian and humanitarian approach, relying on her Catholic faith and years of work representing the children who show up at America's doorsteps to craft bold proposals for immigration reform."

—Camilo Montoya-Galvez, immigration reporter
CBS News

"In *Dignity & Justice*, the stories of immigrant minors open our eyes and hearts to the sometimes common misunderstandings of immigration in the United States. Dakin-Grimm clearly presents reasons why people embark on a search for a better life, despite the suffering entailed by such a long journey. More importantly, *Dignity & Justice* informs us of the Church's teaching on immigration, and furthermore, how to respond when unjust laws impede us to live with equal dignity. Through the author's life experiences, readers are invited to welcome the stranger at our border with open hearts as Jesus welcomed all."

—Sr. Rosalia Meza, VDMF, senior director
Office of Religious Education, Archdiocese of Los Angeles

"Linda Dakin-Grimm brings the careful analysis of a lawyer and the theological sensitivity of the social ethicist to our labyrinthian immigration legislation. Her timely book combines heart-breaking stories of those seeking asylum with reviews of past U.S. exploitation of Central American countries and Church teaching on immigration, not just of Pope Francis but also of his predecessors. Speaking of life issues, she writes, 'Catholics may not oppose abortion and ignore suffering migrants.' Some readers will find this controversial, but her book is deeply rooted in the Catholic tradition."

—Thomas P. Rausch, SJ
Emeritus T. Marie Chilton Professor of Catholic Theology
Loyola Marymount University

DIGNITY
and
JUSTICE

*Welcoming the Stranger
at Our Border*

by

LINDA DAKIN-GRIMM

ORBIS BOOKS
Maryknoll, New York 10545

ORBIS BOOKS
Maryknoll, New York 10545

Fathers and Brothers
MARYKNOLL™

Founded in 1970, Orbis Books endeavors to publish works that enlighten the mind, nourish the spirit, and challenge the conscience. The publishing arm of the Maryknoll Fathers and Brothers, Orbis seeks to explore the global dimensions of the Christian faith and mission, to invite dialogue with diverse cultures and religious traditions, and to serve the cause of reconciliation and peace. The books published reflect the views of their authors and do not represent the official position of the Maryknoll Society. To learn more about Orbis Books, please visit our website at www.orbisbooks.com.

Library of Congress Cataloging-in-Publication Data

Names: Dakin-Grimm, Linda, author.
Title: Dignity and justice : welcoming the stranger at our border / Linda
    Dakin-Grimm.
Description: Maryknoll, New York : Orbis Books, 2020. | Includes
    bibliographical references and index. | Summary: Through stories of
    real children and families, Dignity and Justice explores the issue of
    migration to the southern border of the United States—including
    the historical, social, legal and political dynamics.
Identifiers: LCCN 2020002336 (print) | LCCN 2020002337 (ebook) | ISBN
    9781626983816 (trade paperback) | ISBN 9781608338450 (ebook)
Subjects: LCSH: Emigration and immigration—Religious aspects—Catholic
    Church. | Immigrants—Mexican-American Border Region—Social conditions.
    | Immigrant children—Mexican-American Border Region—Social conditions.
    | United States—Emigration and immigration—History—21st century. |
    United States—Emigration and immigration—Government
    policy—History—21st century. | Immigration enforcement—Social
    conditions—Mexican-American Border Region. | Social justice—Religious
    aspects—Catholic Church. | Christian sociology—Catholic Church.
Classification: LCC BX1795.E44 D35 2020 (print) | LCC BX1795.E44 (ebook)
    | DDC 261.8/380973—dc23
LC record available at https://lccn.loc.gov/2020002336
LC ebook record available at https://lccn.loc.gov/2020002337

To my mom, Gloria Henry Dakin,
my first and best teacher and role model of
diligence, kindness, patience, hospitality, and listening.

And to my husband, Gary Grimm,
my best friend and model of loyalty,
wisdom, curiosity, delight, and wonder.

Contents

Acknowledgments

Many generous people helped and supported me in the work that led to this book. My friends (and real writers) Gennifer Choldenko and Heather King helped me to believe I could write and gave me invaluable concrete feedback in the process. My Mom, Gloria, my husband, Gary, and my friend Jeff Hamilton were my first readers and provided boundless moral support. My editor, Paul McMahon of Orbis, provided wise guidance. Dozens of people support the children and families I represent. They include the talented and tireless legal staffs at Kids in Need of Defense (KIND); Bet Tzedek Legal Services; and Immigrant Defenders Law Center; Jeff Hamilton; Sylvia LeSage; Martha DeLira; Margarita Gonzalez; Yvette Acuna; Araceli Acuna; Silvia Wong; Maria Camacho; Tina Sarafa; Monica Tucker; Audra Steller; Monique Owen; Melissa Fernandez; Patty Dodd; Alvaro Pacheco; Marco Dell'Oro; Lucy Boutte; Bertha Cardenti; Pat Holt; Kathy McQuiggan; Caroline McQuiggan; Ethan McCanless; Kim Venetz; Harriet Rapista; Erick Rubalcava; Raymond Saborio; Jacqueline Marks; Mara Cohen; Allan Marks; Rabbi Jocee Hudson; Federico Bustamante; Marty, Matt, John, and Nicky Sarafa; and Mark and Laura Scarsi. The members of the Southern California Catholic Task Force on Immigration, led by Msgr. Jarlath Cunnane, Isaac Cuevas, A. J. Joven, and David DeMers, provided invaluable support and inspiration. The theology faculty at Loyola Marymount University, specifically professors Cecelia Gonzalez-Andrieu, Matthew Petrusek, Tracy Tiemeier, Daniel Smith-Christopher, Douglas Christie, James Fredericks, Amir Hussain, Jeffrey Siker, David Sanchez, Jonathan Rothchild, and Charlotte Radler, deeply affected my life and my understanding of the response owed to migrants by people of faith. Finally, Bishop David G. O'Connell was instrumental in setting me on this path. He has supported me and the children at every step of the journey. All errors are mine.

Introduction

This book is about migrants who are suffering at the southern border of the United States in the twenty-first century. It is about *who* these people are and *why* they continue to come, even when the current leadership of the United States is doing everything possible to discourage their journeys and turn them away. It is about the hurdles these people face in the U.S. legal system. And it is about presenting the "Catholic way" of thinking about migration and what all Christians are called to do in response to these newcomers.

As a lawyer for more than thirty years, I have represented financial institutions and corporations of one sort or another in disputes against other similar parties. I did this in courts all over the country and have been paid well for doing it. I live in a safe beach town outside of Los Angeles with clean water, fresh air, and excellent local services. I have never had to run from a life-and-death situation or consider emigrating. Living in multicultural Southern California, I felt no hostility toward migrants, but in truth, I rarely thought about them at all. That changed when I met and started working with migrant children.

Children, with and without their parents, have been coming to the United States requesting help for generations. For much of the twentieth century, when the number of children arriving was smaller, they were mostly ignored by the press and the public. Before the 1980s, most unaccompanied children—a legal term that refers to migrant children who arrive without a parent or guardian—actually came from Europe, Asia, and Cuba. In the 1990s, most unaccompanied children came to the United States from Mexico. Over the past ten years, the majority has come from Central America. Hundreds of thousands of desperate Central American family groups have also come to the border in this period.

In the summer of 2014, images in the press of thousands of unaccompanied children at the border briefly captured the American public's attention. That summer, the press reported heavily on the arrival of almost seventy thousand children arriving without parents. The arrival of these children was dubbed "the surge." Some Americans, moved by the photos, wanted to help the children. Others lined the roads of American border towns on which the buses full of children in custody traveled holding signs reading, "Return to sender" and "Go back to Mexico."[1] This was undoubtedly confusing to the children on the buses, as most were from Guatemala, El Salvador, and Honduras.

I saw the press coverage of the surge in 2014 and wondered why so many children would flood the border without their parents. I was curious about what the children wanted. Silently, I was judgmental about why their parents would have allowed this to happen. But I was in the middle of two big cases on opposite coasts, and I looked away. It was someone else's problem.

In 2015, the number of unaccompanied children fell to forty thousand, but in 2016, it rose again to almost sixty thousand, again mostly from Central America.[2] I am a Catholic follower of Jesus Christ. But in my mostly white, affluent Catholic parish, I had never heard a Sunday homily that even mentioned the word "immigration," much less the phenomenon of these unaccompanied children. I struggled to make sense of what Jesus asks of his followers, what our church actually teaches about immigration, and the silence of my own particular community. Some priests from parishes with similar demographics as mine candidly told me that they didn't preach on the subject of immigration because it is "sensitive," and they didn't want to offend parishioners who oppose a welcome but are generous on other issues.

---

1. Halimah Abdullah, "Not in My Backyard: Communities Protest Surge of Immigrant Kids," CNN Politics, July 16, 2014, https://www.cnn.com.

2. Pamela Lizette Cruz and Tony Payan, "Alone and Vulnerable: Unaccompanied Minors in the United States and Mexico," *Rice University's Baker Institute for Public Policy Report* (Houston: Rice University, 2018), 3.

I took on my first pro bono case for an unaccompanied immigrant child in 2015, through the nonprofit agency called Kids in Need of Defense (KIND). KIND's mission is to find and mentor private sector lawyers willing to represent unaccompanied children in court, without charge. This first case with this child led me to another and then to dozens more. At the end of 2015, I gave up my business-law practice to represent unaccompanied children full time, through KIND and other nonprofit agencies like it. I am deeply grateful that my law firm allowed me to do this volunteer legal work from their offices and with the support of the staff.

Immigration issues were front and center during the 2016 presidential campaign in which Donald Trump ran on an anti-immigrant, nationalist "America First" platform, and calling Mexican immigrants the "worst of the worst," "rapists," and "criminals," and then appending that "some" may be good people. The Trump campaign was fueled by the mantra: "Build the wall." In the Trump administration's first year, unable actually to change immigration law, which requires action by Congress, the White House began announcing policies aimed at reducing immigration without congressional approval. In 2017, the number of unaccompanied children arriving at the southern border fell to forty-one thousand. But the next year, it was back up to fifty thousand; and it exploded in 2019, when 63,624 unaccompanied children arrived in just the first six months of the year.[3]

As the anti-immigrant rhetoric amplified in the Trump era, many other lawyers in my firm joined me in taking on children' cases without charge. KIND worked with the Archdiocese of Los Angeles to train a group of nonlawyer volunteers, many from my own parish, who translate, mentor, encourage, befriend, or simply accompany the children we represent. The children our little team has taken on have been supported in these ways by high school students, priests, grandmothers, a rabbi, law students, moms and dads, Bar Mitzvah youth, Eagle Scouts, a bishop, and the members of the Southern

---

3. U.S. Customs and Border Patrol, "U.S. Border Patrol Southwest Border Apprehensions by Sector, Fiscal Year 2019," https://www.cbp.gov.

California Catholic Task Force on immigration. All of us want to welcome children.

Over the past five years, increasing numbers of family groups have also made the long trek north from Central America. In 2014, the year of the children's surge, sixty-eight thousand family groups also came to the southern border, seeking permission to live and work in the United States. An additional seventy-seven thousand families arrived in 2016, Barack Obama's last year in office. During 2017, Donald Trump's first year in office, despite the immediate and continuous roll-out of explicit policies and unwritten strategies aimed at pulling in the welcome mat, the number of new families arriving at the border remained steady at seventy-five thousand.

The Trump administration grew frustrated at the continuous arrival of migrants, notwithstanding its strategies. During the summer of 2018, then attorney general Jeff Sessions, a professed Christian, announced a policy of "zero tolerance." This policy was not, as has been suggested, a continuation from prior administrations, which occasionally had to separate children from adults suspected of serious crimes. Under the new Sessions policy, *all adults* who approached the border with their children to ask for asylum would be forcibly separated from the children, charged with the crime of unlawful entry, and swiftly deported. Their children would be reclassified as unaccompanied, and sent to juvenile detention centers. Mr. Sessions publicly justified the new separation policy by citing the Bible. He argued that "illegal entry into the United States is a crime," and that in Romans 13, the apostle Paul commanded that people obey the laws of the government because God has ordained laws for the purpose of order.[4] Of course, approaching the United States' border to seek asylum is not, and has never been, a crime.

Across the political spectrum, the American public hated family separation. Mr. Sessions' policy was ultimately halted by a federal court, as will be discussed later. But while the separations were in full swing, even more desperate families continued to arrive at the

---

4. Sam Hodges, "Sessions Criticized for 'Zero Tolerance' Bible Quote," *United Methodist News*, June 15, 2018, https://www.umnews.org.

border. The total number of families arriving in 2018 increased dramatically over the previous years to 107,000. And in just the first half of 2019, 390,000 families sought entry at the southern border, a 469 percent increase over 2018.[5]

Who are these people? Why are they so desperate to flee their home countries that they leave everything and everyone they know behind? Why are they willing to travel thousands of miles over dangerous territory, risking their lives? Why do they continue to come, when the United States has made it clear that they are not welcome? Are these people in real danger in their own countries? Or are they perfectly fine, and simply looking for economic opportunities? Are they sympathetic, suffering strangers or lawbreakers, who refuse to honor borders or wait in line? Doesn't the Catholic Church teach that protecting borders and enforcing the civil law are honorable things to do? Do Americans owe anything to these people? Has this country played any role in creating the conditions that make living in their countries dangerous and difficult?

These are the questions addressed in this book. The children and "separated" families I have encountered have changed my perspective and, indeed, my life. They have opened my eyes and my heart. Their stories of daily courage inspire me. They remind me what it felt like to be a child, with aspirations and dreams (and goofy ideas), but with no practical knowledge of how to make dreams happen. They teach me in ways that words never could that all of us have equal dignity. They show me that if we welcome them and give just a little bit of help, in whatever ways we can, they will contribute their own talents and big hearts to our community. This book introduces some of them to you.

Beyond addressing *who* is coming to the southern border, and *why* they are coming, I also discuss the "Catholic way" of thinking about and responding to immigration issues and, in fact, all moral issues. Many people with strong opinions about immigrants, borders, and "the law" have no idea of what U.S. immigration law actually

---

5. U.S. Customs and Border Patrol, "U.S. Border Patrol Southwest Border Apprehensions by Sector, Fiscal Year 2019," https://www.cbp.gov.

provides or how the system presently works. I have also come to understand that many Catholics have no idea what our church has long taught about migration, how Catholic teaching relates to U.S. law and the legal system, and what Catholics are called to do when laws are unjust.

This book summarizes the timeless teachings of our Catholic faith, including how to wrestle with difficult moral questions and, specifically, why our church teaches that we must welcome suffering migrants. Finally, I examine how U.S. law could be changed and propose a concrete, Catholic-faith-informed "comprehensive U.S. immigration reform"—the unicorn everyone says we need, but no one defines.

The children and families I work for and love are not a "social problem." They are very much our brothers and sisters. Their well-being, futures, and indeed salvation are inextricably intertwined with our own. This includes those of us who are fortunate to be able to live contentedly in the places where we were born. Archbishop Jose Gomez of Los Angeles has repeatedly said that immigration is the most urgent human rights issue of our time. In a 2019 homily, he proclaimed, "In Jesus Christ, every barrier, every wall falls down. There is no Mexican, no Vietnamese, no Korean, or Filipino; no Russian or Venezuelan, no migrant or native-born. In Jesus Christ, we are all children of God, made in his image."[6]

Like us, migrants have needs and aspirations, feelings, yearnings, and the desire to know and love God. We are all humans of equal dignity. My hope and prayer is that meeting some of these real people will help your heart to open wider. I pray that together we can cultivate generosity and hospitality, and the willingness to follow the teaching of our faith.

---

6. Archbishop Jose Gomez, homily at 2019 Mass in Recognition of All Immigrants at the Los Angeles Cathedral of Our Lady of the Angels, September 7, 2019.

PART I

GILBERTO

The Holy Family, Jesus, Mary and Joseph, living in exile in Egypt, are... for all times and all places, *the models and protectors of every migrant, alien and refugee of whatever kind who, whether compelled by fear of persecution or by want, is forced to leave his native land, his beloved parents and relatives, his close friends and to seek a foreign soil.*

—Pope Pius XII, *Exsul Familia*,
an apostolic constitution, August 1, 1952

1

Gilberto's Story

I can't sell drugs for you. I'm a Christian. It's against what I believe.

—Fourteen-year-old Gilberto to an MS-13 gang member holding a gun to his chest (2014)

Gilberto was born in Guatemala City in 2000. He doesn't remember his mother, who abandoned him and his father, Santiago, when Gilberto was only a year old. For the first five years of his life, Gilberto lived with Santiago, his paternal grandparents, and his uncle Nelson in Mixco, a city near the capital of Guatemala City but separated by canyons.

Santiago, who walks with a cane, is a bearded, heavy-set man with glasses. He left Guatemala in 2005—when Gilberto was five years old—to find work so that he could support his young son and his parents. Santiago left Gilberto, a slim boy with large dark eyes, in the care of his grandparents and his uncle Nelson. After Santiago left, Gilberto held tightly to a few fond memories of his dad, like the day trip they took to see a small traveling circus. Santiago crossed the border into the United States undetected and found construction work in California. He is one of the million or so Los Angelenos who do not have legal permission to reside in the United States but who nevertheless do the jobs others reject, like washing and parking cars, laboring in construction, working in restaurants, and taking care of our children, homes, and gardens.

Gilberto loves his extended family in Guatemala, but he felt alone there with no parents to care for him. After his father left Guatemala, Gilberto kept in touch with him as much as he could, via phone and WhatsApp. But he never wanted to make his dad feel bad, so he usually didn't tell Santiago how much he was really suffering.

Santiago's own father—Gilberto's grandfather—was murdered when Gilberto was seven years old. He and his wife had gone to a neighborhood ATM to withdraw some cash and were walking home one evening. Just as they reached their home, they were confronted by a gunman. The grandfather managed to push Gilberto's grandmother into the house, but he was shot and killed. The gunman took the money and escaped. No police came to the scene. The despairing family went to the police station themselves to report the crime and beg for help, but the police still did not come to the scene. They never investigated the murder, and the killer was never found.

After the murder, Gilberto's family joined an evangelical Christian church. They all found solace there. Santiago joined the church in Los Angeles too. Gilberto's uncle Isaac, who lived nearby, eventually gave up his factory job and became a pastor in this denomination. Isaac founded a church at his parents' house, where Gilberto lived with his grandmother and his other uncle, Nelson. "I found the peace I needed in the church," Gilberto said. The loving community that gathered at the church in the home he lived in became the center of Gilberto's young life. When Gilberto was nine years old, he was baptized in a nearby river by his uncle Isaac and surrounded by his church friends. Gilberto is proud that he was baptized only after he had demonstrated that he understood what he was doing and that baptism was his own choice.

The Gangs

As he grew, Gilberto became increasingly public with his faith. He became more involved in the church and especially its outreach to youth at risk of being targeted by the gangs that plagued their community. Gilberto joined a troop of young people who taught the youngest children to avoid gang life and to surrender their lives to Jesus Christ. The troop practiced and performed Christian skits and versions of folk tales, like Little Red Riding Hood, for the children, and they posted videos of their performances on YouTube. Gilberto liked acting and was proud to demonstrate his faith in public. He became well known in the community for his strong faith and for his witness to other children. Gilberto explained that the gang called Mara Salvatrucha, or MS-13, is particularly interested in attracting very young children because "young kids . . . don't always understand what they are doing and they can easily be manipulated into doing things like selling drugs or even killing people, but the gang won't have any consequences from the little kids' actions." Gilberto said he participated in the acting troupe to "stand up for Jesus Christ" by "getting in their way."

MS-13 is one of two dominant gangs that terrorize ordinary people in Guatemala. Its main rival is Mara 18, sometimes called the 18th Street gang. The two gangs fight each other for territory in Guatemala, El Salvador, and Honduras. Today, both MS-13 and Mara 18 are international criminal gangs, but they were originally formed on the streets of Los Angeles, California, in the 1980s, by young men who had escaped from civil wars in Central America, only to encounter the gang culture of the Crips and Bloods, then prevailing in the poorest areas of Los Angeles. The United States exported MS-13 and Mara 18 back to Central America when it deported the earliest members of these gangs to their countries in the 1990s.

MS-13 controlled Gilberto's neighborhood. Its members became increasingly angry about the anti-gang and outreach programs at Uncle Isaac's church, because the programs for youths interfered with gang priorities and activities. MS-13 members retaliated brutally, both by trying to force Gilberto, the pastor's nephew, to abandon his church and work for them, and by terrorizing the entire church.

Gilberto had always enjoyed learning, attending school regularly and achieving good grades. He never got into any trouble at school. He attended a public school that was primarily for low-income students. But MS-13 had seduced many students in this school. When Gilberto was just ten years old, MS-13 members barged into a school assembly and began throwing rocks at Gilberto and the classmates sitting near him. One friend was hit on the head and hurt badly enough to be taken to the hospital. Following the attack, an older MS-13 member cornered Gilberto outside and told him that if he didn't start selling "sweets" (drugs), they would hurt him. After that, Gilberto was on high alert, careful not to be alone for the rest of the year. He didn't tell his father or his grandmother what was happening.

At age eleven, Gilberto was again cornered by MS-13–affiliated youth in a classroom at school. This time, they beat him badly and only stopped when a teacher and other students came into the room. Then, they casually sauntered out. Although some of the attackers were students at the school and their identities were well known, the school did nothing to punish them because the administrators and teachers themselves were terrified of gang members. Later that year, Gilberto was walking in his neighborhood when he heard gunshots, which was not an uncommon occurrence. Minutes later, he came upon the body of a sixteen-year-old boy who had been shot dead in the street. Gilberto didn't know the boy, but he stared at the body in grief and shock. Before he realized it, the same gang member who had threatened him at the school assembly was standing next to him, whispering in his ear that, now, Gilberto would sell drugs for MS-13, or he would be the next boy lying dead in the street.

After this, Gilberto was too afraid to return to school. He finally told his grandmother what was happening. She arranged for him to attend a Christian school in a different neighborhood. Gilberto's older cousin drove him to and from the new school. But this Christian school was for working adults. Classes were only held on Saturdays. Gilberto was one of only two children permitted to attend. During the week, Gilberto stayed inside the house that doubled as his uncle Isaac's church. MS-13 members regularly hung out on the street corner outside.

In the absence of parents, Gilberto clung to his faith and to his church community. He continued to participate in his youth group. But MS-13 tormented the entire congregation. Gang members burst into prayer meetings in the church, disrupted services, terrorized participants, and threw around the furniture. One time, the children found a litter of puppies with their paws cut off, bleeding to death on the church doorstep, that they immediately understood to be symbolic of themselves. They regularly found spoiled food and feces thrown on the doorstep. As pastor, Gilberto's uncle Isaac wrote to the police begging for protection for his flock. The police responded politely to these letters, but they never protected the congregation because the police were outmanned and under constant threat from MS-13 gang members.

After a year at the Saturday-only school, Gilberto, now thirteen years old, transferred to a regular high school that met all day, every weekday. Gilberto and his grandmother had hoped that, because Gilberto had not been bothered at the Saturday school, he would be allowed to attend high school in peace. They were wrong. Just one month into his new school year, MS-13 members began to stalk Gilberto on his way home from school. They taunted and tripped him as he walked. They grabbed and destroyed his books and school supplies. They told him they would kill him if he didn't sell drugs for them. Gilberto actually told his attackers that he was a Christian and that it was wrong to sell drugs. They laughed at him. He managed to get away from them several times by darting into a store or into a group of people. He didn't tell his grandmother or uncle Isaac.

In early 2014, MS-13 members shot and killed the father of one of Gilberto's friends. Soon after that, when Gilberto was still thirteen, four MS-13 members grabbed him and pulled him into an alley after school. One of them put a gun to Gilberto's chest, quietly telling him that he had been warned repeatedly, and now he would die. As he said this, a door to a store full of people opened at the end of the alley and people began spilling out. The four gang members argued among themselves about whether to shoot Gilberto in front of so many people. Gilberto pled with the men that he could never sell drugs for them because, as a Christian, drugs are against his religion. This made the men angrier; they said that in that case, they would kill Gilberto's uncle Isaac, the pastor, so he couldn't attend church anymore and wouldn't have any more excuses. As the alley continued to fill with people, the gang members allowed Gilberto to slip away. His uncle Isaac later found him huddled at the end of the alley, shaking and terrified. The family knew that Gilberto would have to leave Guatemala to save his own life.

The Migration

Gilberto left his home and traveled through Guatemala and then Mexico for more than a month, on foot and on buses, initially with a guide—a *coyote*—whom his uncle Isaac had paid to help him. The man attended Isaac's church. Gilberto's family hoped that he would be trustworthy. Though he had promised to take Gilberto to the United States border, the man took Gilberto only as far as the Guatemala-Mexico border and turned him over to a stranger. Gilberto was told to call this second coyote, "the General." The General told Gilberto they had to check in with someone in every town they passed through in Mexico, or Gilberto would be tracked and killed. The General told Gilberto that the cartels that control drugs and human migration in that country know who has paid to move through the country.

The General handed Gilberto over to another coyote somewhere in Mexico. This man locked Gilberto up for two weeks while he extorted money from Gilberto's father, Santiago. After Santiago wired money, Gilberto was allowed to continue, reaching the United States border in Texas. The third coyote left Gilberto to cross the border by himself. He gave Gilberto a phone number to call when he reached the U.S. side. In Texas, Gilberto wandered alone until he found a car repair shop with a telephone. He called the number the coyote had given him, believing he would get help finding his father. Gilberto waited for a few hours at the car repair shop. Eventually, a man in a red car came for him. But instead of helping Gilberto, the man drove him to an apartment where he was held hostage, locked in a small room for a month. The man told Gilberto that, if he screamed, the apartment's manager would call him and, if he tried to escape, the residents in the adjacent apartments would turn him in. The man brought food, usually just soup, for Gilberto every few days. He was hungry and dehydrated. The man brought other people to the room and sometimes took people away. At one point, more than ten people were held captive in the room with Gilberto. During this time, Gilberto mostly worried about his father, who had developed epilepsy after a fall at work. Gilberto feared the stress of worrying about him would cause his father to have a seizure.

Gilberto later learned that during the month in which he was held hostage in Texas, his father had received a series of calls from a man who calmly said he would kill Gilberto if Santiago did not wire money. Each time, Santiago sent a money order as directed, but Gilberto was not released. The man would call again and demand more money. Eventually, when the man decided he had extracted all the money he could from Santiago, he simply let Gilberto go. The Texas Highway Patrol found Gilberto wandering disoriented on the highway. They arrested the skinny, confused boy at gunpoint. They handcuffed Gilberto and took him to their station, where he collapsed and was taken by ambulance to a nearby hospital. Upon release from the hospital, the police turned Gilberto over to Immigration and Customs Enforcement (ICE).

ICE sent Gilberto to a detention center for migrant children in Houston run by a private company under contract to the U.S. Department of Health and Human Services' Office of Refugee Resettlement (ORR). At the ORR shelter, Gilberto was finally able to speak with his dad on the telephone, an indescribable relief for them both. Eventually, Santiago signed a contract with ORR, promising to take care of Gilberto and bring him to immigration court hearings, in exchange for gaining custody of Gilberto.

ORR gave Santiago a list of private agencies that might help Gilberto find a pro bono lawyer to represent him in court without charging a fee. However, the contract that Santiago signed stated clearly that if Gilberto couldn't afford a lawyer or find one for free, the government would not provide a lawyer for him. Gilberto would have to go to immigration court without a lawyer.

The Legal Struggle

In Los Angeles, Gilberto lived with his father, his new stepmother, and their two young U.S.-born daughters, who were immediately entranced by their strange older brother, who spoke only Spanish.

Gilberto enrolled in high school and joined a youth group at the family's church. He felt safe with Santiago and his new family, and he was deeply grateful to be able to attend school and church without fear. He couldn't remember ever having felt that way. Santiago knew that he needed to find a lawyer for Gilberto, but the family could not afford one. Having left Gilberto behind in Guatemala once, Santiago was determined to find help for his traumatized son in the United States. He called every agency on the list repeatedly for months while they waited for Gilberto's initial immigration court date. No one was available to take Gilberto's case. Finally, the agency Kids in Need of Defense (KIND) agreed to find a pro bono lawyer for Gilberto, and they did.

Children like Gilberto have been coming to the United States' border unaccompanied by adults for generations. The number of unaccompanied children arriving from Central America increased dramatically and became a phenomenon in the second decade of the twenty-first century. Between October 1, 2013, and September 30, 2014, U.S. Customs and Border Patrol (CBP) apprehended almost seventy thousand unaccompanied children attempting to cross the southern border of the United States. Gilberto was part of this wave of immigration, which was dubbed "the surge." Some children, like Gilberto, were in desperate fear for their lives and hoped to reunite with a family member already in the United States. Others had been abandoned, abused, or neglected by their family in their home country. Still others were starving, their families simply unable to provide for them.

The Obama Presidency

On June 2, 2014, just as Gilberto entered the country, President Barack Obama called the masses of unaccompanied children entering at the southern border an "urgent humanitarian situation." He directed a coordinated federal response under emergency homeland security authorities. Mr. Obama's use of the term "humanitarian" suggested that the response would be one that was aimed at promoting the welfare of the children. On June 30, 2014, while Gilberto was in ORR detention, Mr. Obama sent a letter to congressional leaders seeking emergency funding. But the funding he sought was not to assist the children's integration into this country. Instead, it was for "an aggressive deterrence strategy focused on the removal and repatriation of [the] recent border crossers" like Gilberto, as quickly as possible. Mr. Obama acknowledged a "legal and moral obligation to make sure we appropriately care for unaccompanied children who are apprehended," but only for the time it takes to "quickly return unlawful migrants to their home countries."

In the remaining years of the Obama presidency, the government's strategy was to place unaccompanied children like Gilberto in a fast-track immigration court process, requiring them to prove quickly—often without time to find a lawyer—that they qualified for some kind of exceptional status like asylum or Special Immigrant Juvenile Status (SIJS). The strategy was to deport them swiftly to their places of origin, if they couldn't do so. Gilberto had assumed that his biggest problems were behind him when he was released from the ORR detention center and reunited with his father in Los Angeles. He and Santiago were distressed to learn that the legal bases that might allow him to remain in the United States are narrow, very difficult to prove, and that the burden to prove all the facts was entirely on them.

Two Systems

The first thing Gilberto learned about was the complicated process he would have to navigate to seek permission to remain in the States. His lawyer explained that he would go through two systems at the same time. In federal immigration court, he would have to "plead to the charges" against him and defend himself against being immediately deported. At the same time, he would go to a different federal agency called U.S. Citizenship and Immigration Services (USCIS) to persuade officers there to grant him a humanitarian legal status to stay in the country. USCIS is a federal agency under the Department of Homeland Security (DHS) that administers the immigration system. USCIS is one of the three successor agencies to the old

Immigration and Naturalization Service (INS), which was dissolved when DHS was created after the terrorist events of September 11, 2001.[1]

When Gilberto was released to his father, he was placed in what are called "removal proceedings" in immigration court. "Removal" is the legal term the government started using in the 1990s instead of deportation. It means the same thing. Being placed "in removal proceedings" meant that Gilberto would plead to the charges against him in immigration court. Attorneys who work for DHS would argue that he should be deported. At the same time that this court case was moving forward, Gilberto would need to apply to USCIS for either asylum or special immigrant juvenile status, under the fast-track process for children that the Obama administration created in response to the surge crisis. If Gilberto obtained either status, he could go back to the immigration judge and ask that the removal case against him be ended.

In immigration court, the "charges" against Gilberto were simply that he was not a U.S. citizen and that he didn't have permission to enter the country before he did so. Gilberto had to stand before the judge and admit or deny those facts, in response to the question "How do you plead?" By admitting the facts—and Gilberto had to admit them because they were true—he would be conceding that the United States had the right to deport him. Once Gilberto pled to the charges, he could then ask the judge not to deport him immediately, but instead to give him time to seek asylum or special immigrant juvenile status from USCIS.

Like every unaccompanied migrant child, Gilberto didn't know what USCIS was, much less how to apply for any status there. He didn't know what the requirements were for either status. He knew only that he had suffered terribly in Guatemala, that his life was in jeopardy there, and that he needed to be with his father. Gilberto had assumed that if he told his story to a judge, he would be allowed

---

1. The other two successor agencies are Immigration and Customs Enforcement (ICE), the police force of the immigration system, and Customs and Border Protection (CBP), which replaced the old "Border Patrol."

to remain in this country. He learned that under U.S. law, stories of terrible suffering often do not result in permission to stay.

Gilberto wanted to apply for asylum. He was desperately afraid, and he wanted to be allowed to live safely and freely. But in the law, the term "asylum" does not mean what Gilberto had assumed and what most American people think: "desperate people fleeing really bad circumstances, seeking safety." The United States simply does not grant asylum to most of the people we *know* have suffered terribly and who *we believe* to be genuinely fleeing persecution, poverty, terror, wars, famine, and atrocities.

Five Grounds of Persecution

Gilberto and Santiago learned that asylum is available only to people who can prove they experienced past serious persecution in their homeland (or have a credible fear of future persecution), which Gilberto felt he could do, but then only if they could prove the particular persecution they suffered was "on account of" one of five specific grounds: their race, religion, national origin, political opinion, or membership in a "particular social group." This was a shock to Gilberto, who could not fathom why the United States would care why his persecutors had tormented him. Gilberto had believed that if he actually suffered terribly and was in grave danger, he would be allowed to stay.

Gilberto was also dismayed to learn that to qualify for asylum, the burden of proof would be entirely on him, and that he would need to do more than just tell his story. He would have to offer actual evidence of very severe persecution and of the reasons why his persecutors came after him—called, in legal terms, the "nexus" between the persecution and one of the five protected grounds. Gilberto learned that the government's lawyers would not have to do anything at all in his case, once he admitted that he was not a U.S. citizen and that he had not had permission to come to this country. If Gilberto could not prove that he suffered severe persecution and that his persecutors hurt him because of one of the five grounds, he would not get asylum. Gilberto was confounded to learn that he also had to prove that his own country, Guatemala, couldn't or wouldn't protect him, and that he could not just move away from Mixco to some other place in Guatemala to be safe. Gilberto had no idea how to prove these things. In other words, a child from Guatemala like Gilberto who was severely persecuted by gangs, who was himself beaten and threatened with death, and who has seen family members killed simply will not be granted asylum under U.S. law unless he can prove both that the persecution happened (or is likely to happen) and that it was on account of race, religion, national origin, political opinion, or membership in a "particular social group." The person who answers "I was tormented by gangs because they persecute everyone where I live" will not be granted asylum. Gilberto wondered how someone without a lawyer could ever win asylum.

Gilberto was dismayed to learn that asylum is never available to people who were severely persecuted for some reason other than the five. Likewise, Gilberto and his father had not understood that people who suffer for reasons other than persecution, like famine, natural disaster, severe poverty, war, or lack of medical care—never qualify for asylum—no matter how severe their suffering. But Gilberto was undeterred. He wanted to pursue asylum on the basis that he had experienced severe persecution on account of his evangelical Christian faith in Jesus Christ.

Psychological Evaluation

Gilberto, Santiago, and his pro bono lawyer went to work. It took time for Gilberto to become comfortable enough to tell his painful story. At the same time that he was meeting with his lawyer, Gilberto also met with a licensed mental health clinician, so that she could provide an independent psychological evaluation that he could offer as proof of the trauma he suffered as a result of persecution. In Los Angeles, gifted clinicians at organizations like St. John's Well Child and Family Center, Amanecer Community Counseling Center, and many others provide invaluable free services to children who can't afford them. Gilberto's therapist eventually wrote a report diagnosing him with post-traumatic stress disorder. She explained that his trauma showed itself in persistent symptoms of fear and anxiety. Gilberto's specific symptoms included difficulty with concentration, a hyper-vigilance, a frequent "startle" response, nightmares, fear of being watched in his daily activities, sadness, worry, emotional distance, and depression. The clinician's expert report became part of the evidence in Gilberto's case. It substantiated that he had been severely persecuted because he manifested the kind of trauma symptoms that persecution creates. But he needed more.

Faith Testimony

Gilberto would have to submit his own sworn "declaration," a written statement in which he told his story in his own words "under penalty of perjury." Gilberto's testimony about his experiences, his faith, and the reasons why he had been targeted for persecution were sincere and compelling. Gilberto's lawyer reached out to his uncle Isaac, still the struggling pastor of the church in Mixco, to ask for his written testimony about what happened to Gilberto. Uncle Isaac testified about Gilberto's faith, and that as a Christian, Gilberto had worked with families and children from troubled homes in the congregation, teaching and modeling for them how to avoid gang life and dedicate their lives to Jesus. Isaac testified that Gilberto had received death threats from gangsters because of the work he was doing for his faith. He testified that the persecution of Gilberto and the congregation had happened just as Gilberto said and that even after Gilberto left Guatemala, gang members continued to come by the church looking for him. Isaac testified that after Gilberto escaped, the harassment at the church became so constant and terrifying that he, Isaac, had had a stroke. Isaac provided copies of the letters he had written to the police, and their polite responses that were not accompanied by any action. Isaac "corroborated" Gilberto's testimony that he was persecuted because of his faith, that the police could not or would not help him, and that Gilberto had no family to help him anywhere else in Guatemala.

Gilberto's new pastor in Los Angeles also gave sworn written testimony that Gilberto's faith was real and that he continued to practice it in California. Gilberto's local pastor affirmed that Gilberto joined the church as soon as he arrived in Los Angeles, that he was active in the church's youth ministry, and that he is "a

good Christian who has obeyed the Word of God in extremely difficult circumstances." Gilberto's lawyer gathered evidence about the
conditions in Guatemala that made it impossible for him to return
or live safely anywhere in that country. Finally, his lawyer wrote a
lengthy legal brief, explaining why, under U.S. law, the facts of Gilberto's case qualified him for asylum.

The Outcome

Gilberto presented all of his evidence for asylum to USCIS under
the Obama-era fast-track procedures for unaccompanied children.
This process was intended to be a much less adversarial, and more
age-appropriate, process than seeking asylum in a trial in immigration court.[2] All of Gilberto's evidence was submitted to USCIS in
December 2015. A USCIS asylum officer interviewed Gilberto just
after Christmas that same year. Gilberto was required to bring his
own translator, who was a Spanish-speaking volunteer from the
Archdiocese of Los Angeles.

At the USCIS office, the officer carefully questioned Gilberto for
about three hours, painstakingly inquiring about every line of his
written declaration and those of his uncle and his pastor.

At the end of the interview, the officer told Gilberto to come
back in ten days to learn whether he would be granted asylum.
This was the normal timing and procedure for minors in 2015. The
interviewer told Gilberto that if his application was not approved,
he could seek asylum in a trial before the judge, who was in charge

---

2. In May 2019, the Trump administration announced that children who
come to the United States unaccompanied but are later released to a sponsor
would no longer be considered "unaccompanied" and would no longer be eligible
for the USCIS asylum process that Gilberto used. Instead, the Trump administration would treat them as adults in an adversarial trial in immigration court.
On July 1, 2019, lawyers from KIND, Catholic Legal Immigration Network
(CLINIC), Public Counsel, and a private law firm (all acting pro bono) filed a
lawsuit in federal court in Maryland against DHS and USCIS, seeking to enjoin
this new Trump administration policy. Judge George Hazel blocked the administration's intended action on August 2, 2019, pending full resolution of the case at
trial. The case is ongoing.

of his case in immigration court. Several days later, the asylum officer advised that Gilberto should not return to the office to receive a decision—it would be sent in the mail. Gilberto waited. About three months later, Gilberto received a letter informing him that he had been granted asylum, effective March 2016. Gilberto was ecstatic and grateful to God.

Today, Gilberto is a tall, slim, confident nineteen-year-old. He speaks English fluently, and sometimes he smiles broadly. He graduated from high school in June 2019 and has enlisted in the U.S. military. He will proudly serve his newly adopted country as a U.S. Marine. After a year with asylum status, Gilberto applied to USCIS to "adjust status" from asylee to "lawful permanent resident" (LPR), commonly known as a green-card holder. Gilberto received his green card in November 2017. He will be eligible to apply for citizenship in 2021.

2

The Background

Why was life so difficult for Gilberto and his family in Guatemala? Why did Gilberto need to flee Guatemala? Why did the Guatemalan police ignore the murder of Gilberto's grandfather and the terrorizing of Uncle Isaac's church? Why would teachers ignore violence against young students in school? Why are criminal gangs allowed to menace ordinary people with impunity? Has the United States played any role in creating the desperate situations presently faced by ordinary children and families in Guatemala? The answers to all of these questions start more than a hundred years before Gilberto was born with Guatemala's history.

United States and Guatemala

The United States' involvement in Guatemala dates back to the late 1800s, when Americans discovered a voracious taste for bananas and the invention of the refrigerated steamship made transporting produce over long distances possible. Today, "colonialism" is recognized as having been the wrongful taking of other people's land and property and the ignorant trampling of indigenous cultures. Americans pride ourselves on never having been colonizers. Our country's self-image is the proud nation that shook off the bonds of British colonization. But there are more ways to "colonize" than formally to declare another land to be yours.

The United Fruit Company

In December 1904, President Theodore Roosevelt announced to the world that the United States had the right to intervene in the economic affairs of small countries in Central America and the Caribbean. Roosevelt claimed that his economic interventionist policy was born of a desire to see these small countries "stable, orderly and prosperous." As a practical matter, Roosevelt placed the U.S. military at the disposal of American businesses with financial interests in the region. These businesses desired stability so that their economic interests would prosper. In the early 1900s, Teddy Roosevelt coined the expression "speak softly but carry a big stick," in a famous speech, describing his willingness for the U.S. military to protect American business interests in the region.[1] Roosevelt placed the U.S. military at the disposal of, among others, a New Orleans–based business called the United Fruit Company, to protect its growing commercial interests in Guatemala and throughout Central America. Indeed, the U.S. State Department's website still describes the regular American military interventions in Central American countries in the 1900s that occurred whenever the United States perceived a need to "restore internal stability." Roosevelt's interventionist approach was dubbed "gunboat diplomacy."

Between the late 1890s and the 1920s, with the U.S. military as the "big stick," the United Fruit Company gained significant control of Guatemala's resources. At the same time, the United States became Guatemala's leading trading partner.[2] In 1901, the Guatemalan government hired United Fruit to manage the country's postal service. In 1913, United Fruit created the Tropical Radio and Telegraph Company. By 1930, United Fruit had absorbed more than twenty rival firms and had become the largest employer in all of Central America. It controlled 63 percent of the Central American banana market and had its "tentacles" in every power structure in the region. United Fruit was able to set prices and taxes, and dictate

---

1. "President Roosevelt's Speech on the Monroe Doctrine, Advocates Building and Maintaining a Large and Well Equipped Navy as the Best Means of Having It Respected, 'Speak Softly and Carry a Big Stick,' Is the Motto He Used in Illustrating His Point with Good Effect," *Arizona Journal-Miner* (April 3, 1905): 1, https://chroniclingamerica.loc.gov.

2. Stephen M. Streeter, *Managing the Counterrevolution: The United States and Guatemala, 1954–1961* (Athens, GA: Ohio University Press, 2000), 8.

employee treatment, free from local government intervention. By the early 1950s, United Fruit and other U.S. businesses controlled Guatemala's primary electrical utilities, its only railroad, and the banana industry, which provided Guatemala's chief agricultural export.[3]

A "Banana Republic"

Because U.S. investors were unnerved by Central America's frequent internal wars, military coups, and the rise and fall of *caudillos* (strongmen), the United States continued—long after Teddy Roosevelt left office—to protect American interests by "stabilizing" the region.[4] In 1954, at the height of the Cold War, the Eisenhower administration engineered the overthrow of the democratically elected government of Guatemala, in the guise of "fighting communism," a story that has been well documented by historians.[5] They did this because, in the ten preceding years, Guatemalan citizens, weary of foreign control of their jobs, their land, and their country, had sought to weaken the grip of United Fruit. Guatemalans had elected a government that had promised to reclaim foreign-controlled land for Guatemalans. Under the guise of "fighting communism," then deputy director of the CIA Allen Dulles and his brother, U.S. secretary of state John Foster Dulles, orchestrated a coup to unseat elected Guatemalan president Jacobo Arbenz Guzman and to install a puppet dictator, Carlos Castillo Armas, who was willing to defer to American interests.

The derogatory term "banana republic" was coined to refer to places like Guatemala, whose leaders were directly beholden to American business interests and subservient to U.S. military might. American intervention in Central America throughout the twentieth century protected U.S. business interests at the expense of local peoples. As Greg Grandin, Yale University professor of history and the author of many noted books including *The Last Colonial Mas-*

---

3. Ibid., 8–9.
4. Ibid., 9.
5. See, e.g., ibid.; and Greg Grandin, *The Last Colonial Massacre: Latin America in the Cold War* (Chicago: University of Chicago Press, 2004).

sacre explains, even more than Cuba, Guatemala was the "staging ground" for the U.S. cold war against perceived communism.[6]

Civil War

Following the Dulles brothers' coup, ordinary Guatemalans were enraged at having had their election subverted. A bloody, thirty-six-year-long civil war ensued, from 1960 to 1996, in which Guatemalans resisted the U.S.-installed, corrupt leadership. United States' tax dollars supported the government's military and police forces against the people, who were labeled "communists." Scholars estimate that two hundred thousand Guatemalans were killed or "disappeared" during this long war, and that more than one million people were displaced. All sides in the war resorted to extreme violence, terror, death squads, and recruitment of child soldiers.

American University professor Anthony W. Fontes, an expert on the culture, history, method, and evolution of violence and insecurity in Guatemala, explains that during the long civil war, the Guatemalan police functioned as an extension of the military—badly corrupting the police in the process. The Guatemalan police engaged in illegal detentions, threats, extrajudicial killings, kidnappings, and disappearances, often for profit. The U.N. Truth and Reconciliation Commission for Guatemala concluded that the vast majority of victims in the thirty-six-year civil war were noncombatants, and that U.S.-supported, trained, and funded government security forces and progovernment paramilitaries were responsible for 93 percent of the deaths.[7]

The Emergence of Gangs

Not surprisingly, waves of "displaced" Guatemalans fled the violence and terror during the civil war. Those who made it to the United States often settled in the poorest sections of big cities. In

---

6. Grandin, *The Last Colonial Massacre*, 4.

7. *Memoria de Silencio,* United Nations Office of Protective Services, June 1999; Kirsten Weld, *Paper Cadavers: The Archives of Dictatorship in Guatemala* (Durham, NC: Duke University Press, 2014).

Los Angeles, such migrants encountered the L.A. street culture of the prominent African American street gangs, the Bloods and the Crips, and their Latino counterpart, *La Eme*. They formed their own street gangs—MS-13 (Mara Salvatrucha) and Mara 18 (the 18th Street gang), named for specific streets in Los Angeles, emulating L.A. street culture.[8] In the 1990s, as the Guatemalan civil war was coming to an end, the United States deported busloads of MS-13 and 18th Street gang members back to Central America. They took to a Guatemala decimated by decades of war, expertise in extortion, drug running, and gang warfare that they had learned on the streets of L.A. The *Maras* have since evolved into sophisticated, ultraviolent networks that practically control large swaths of Guatemala, El Salvador, and Honduras and terrorize their ordinary citizens with impunity.[9]

Meanwhile, around the world, the Berlin Wall fell and the U.S.S.R. dissolved in 1991. A peace accord in the Guatemalan civil war was signed in 1996. As the perceived threat of communism waned, so did U.S. interest in Central America. But after four

---

8. See "MS-13 Gang: The Story behind One of the World's Most Brutal Street Gangs," BBC News, April 19, 2017, https://www.bbc.com; and "MS13," Insight Crime, March 11, 2019, https://www.insightcrime.org.

9. Tal Kopan and David Shortell, "MS-13 Is Trump's Public Enemy No. 1, but Should It Be?," CNN Politics, updated April 29, 2017, http://www.cnn.com; Albert De Amicis, "Mara Salvatrucha (MS-13) and Its Violent World," University of Pittsburgh Graduate School for Public and International Affairs, October 9, 2010, https://www.ncjrs.gov/pdffiles1/239226.pdf; U.S. Department of State, "Guatemala 2017 Crime and Safety Report," April 10, 2017, https://www.osac. gov; Clare Ribando Seelke, Congressional Research Service, "Gangs in Central America," February 20, 2014, https://digital.library.unt.edu; Maureen Taft-Morales, Congressional Research Service, "Guatemala: Political, Security, and Socio-Economic Conditions and U.S. Relations 2," August 7, 2014 ("The intimidation of judicial officials, widespread corruption, and the involvement of organized crime in violence and extortion are all widely seen as contributing to high levels of impunity and public mistrust in institutions."); Freedom in the World—Guatemala, Freedom House, https://www.freedomhouse.org ("The judiciary is hobbled by corruption, inefficiency, capacity shortages, and the intimidation of judges and prosecutors. . . . Police are accused of torture, extortion, kidnapping, extrajudicial killings, and drug-related crimes").

decades of civil war, Guatemala was left with two disabling challenges. First, a brain drain had occurred during the war, as educated people and those with money fled the country. Second, Guatemala was left with an entrenched government culture of corruption and a deeply corrupt police force. The criminal gangs born in L.A. strolled back into this broken situation.

In the two decades since the end of the civil war, the gangs have partnered with successive waves of corrupt governments, aided by the supposedly "reformed" Guatemalan National Civil Police (PNC), considered today to be among the most corrupt and criminal police forces in the Western Hemisphere. Ordinary Guatemalans, like Gilberto's family, simply have no real access to police protection from crime. They live in constant fear, trying to stay off the radar of both gangs *and* the police—with nowhere to turn when extortion demands begin or lives are threatened or taken. Professor Fontes of the American University observes that less than 5 percent of violent crime in Guatemala today is even prosecuted. Until and unless the deep and pervasive corruption in the Guatemalan government is rooted out and the PNC fundamentally and structurally is reformed—a goal, which currently seems to be impossible—there will be no peace or security for ordinary families and children like Gilberto.

Anti-Corruption Efforts

Has anything improved since the end of the civil war in 1996? Sadly, little real progress seems to have been made.

In 2006, during the presidency of George W. Bush, Guatemala agreed to a groundbreaking anti-corruption effort with a U.N.-backed group called the International Commission against Impunity in Guatemala (CICIG). The CICIG's purpose was to provide external assistance to Guatemalan prosecutors and the PNC in rooting out and prosecuting corruption within government structures. CICIG personnel were specifically tasked with identifying secret and clandestine security forces and identifying illegal links between government officials and police, on the one hand, and gangs and organized crime on the other.

The Bush administration strongly backed the CICIG. The Obama administration continued to support it. Among U.N. contributors, the United States has been the top donor to the CICIG since its founding, providing over $44 million in support over the years.[10] The idea behind the CICIG was that a corrupt system simply cannot ferret out corruption inside itself. Therefore, to defeat corruption, the CICIG provided teams of international lawyers to co-prosecute serious government and police corruption cases, alongside Guatemalan prosecutors. The presence and experience of the international co-prosecutors reduced the opportunity for bribes and pay-offs to derail prosecutions. The CICIG enjoyed broad international support to help Guatemala truly root out entrenched corruption. Change seemed to be possible. But it was not to last.

The Current Situation

In 2015, Guatemala's then president Otto Perez Molina, a retired military intelligence officer, was caught in a serious corruption scandal. Guatemalan voters—hungry for major change to the culture of corruption and violence—went for something completely different, electing TV comic Jimmy Morales as their new president. Mr. Morales, whose campaign slogan was "not corrupt or a thief," was an entertainer, not a politician. At age forty-six, he was famous for performing in blackface and for having once played a lowly farmer who accidentally became president.

In 2017, less than two years later, Mr. Morales (whose campaign had secretly been supported by the same military and police figures who had backed his predecessor) faced a corruption scandal of his own. CICIG prosecutors accused Morales of having accepted nearly one million dollars of illegal funds. His older brother and close advisor, Samuel Morales, and one of his adult sons, Jose Morales, were arrested on corruption and money-laundering charges. Thousands of Guatemalans called for Morales to step down. He refused.

10. Mary Beth Sheridan, "How U.S. Apathy Helped Kill a Pioneering Anti-corruption Campaign in Guatemala," *Washington Post*, June 14, 2019, https://www.washingtonpost.com.

Instead, Mr. Morales announced that he would end the CICIG. His foreign minister expelled the Colombian commissioner of the CICIG, Ivan Velasquez, from the country. Mr. Morales also turned to the Trump administration for help in muzzling the CICIG. He accompanied intense lobbying with obsequious public gestures toward Mr. Trump. Two days after Mr. Trump's controversial December 2017 decision to move the U.S. embassy in Israel from Tel Aviv to Jerusalem, Mr. Morales loudly endorsed the move and subsequently flew to Jerusalem himself on a jet provided by Trump ally and billionaire Sheldon Adelson to open Guatemala's own embassy there.[11] Mr. Trump himself met with Mr. Morales, and the *Washington Post* reported that the Guatemalan diplomats in the United States hosted the president's son-in-law and advisor, Jared Kushner, at a lavish dinner in this period.[12]

Mr. Morales's efforts worked. The Trump administration froze U.S. aid for CICIG, and the program ended in September 2019.[13] On his way out of office, Mr. Morales signed a so-called "safe third country" agreement with the Trump administration that would allow the Trump administration swiftly to deport from the United States asylum-seeking migrants from Honduras and El Salvador *to Guatemala*. The agreement was swiftly ruled unconstitutional by the Guatemalan Supreme Court. Morales's term as president ended at year-end 2019.

On September 11, 2019, the U.S. Supreme Court overturned a preliminary injunction by California District Court judge Jon Tigar that would have enjoined the enforcement of the Trump administration's announced policy of denying entry to seek asylum *to anyone* who passed through another country on the way to the United States, as do migrants from Guatemala, without asking for (and being denied) asylum in the country they passed through. The Supreme Court's decision was only about the preliminary

---

11. Jeffrey Heller and Dan Williams, "Guatemala Opens Embassy in Jerusalem, Two Days after U.S. Move," Reuters, May 16, 2018, https://www.reuters.com.

12. Sheridan, "U.S. Apathy."

13. Ibid.

injunction. It did not include reasoning, and it was not "on the merits"—meaning that the case challenging the Trump administration's policy will continue in the San Francisco District Court. But while the case progresses, the administration is free to enforce its restrictive policy. The effect significantly reduces the numbers of people from Guatemala who may even ask for asylum.

In the months leading to the August 2019 general election for a new Guatemalan president, two of the top three contenders (one of whom had worked closely with the CICIG) were barred from running, and another candidate was arrested in the United States on drug trafficking and weapons charges. Neither of the remaining two candidates committed to restarting the CICIG if elected. Candidate Alejandro Giammattei, running in his fourth election, was the director of Guatemala's prison system from 2006 to 2008. Just one year into that job, Guatemalan prosecutors had accused Giammattei of carrying out extrajudicial killings, after the police killed seven inmates while trying to regain control of a prison he supervised. He was acquitted of that charge. The CICIG and the Guatemalan Public Ministry accused the other candidate, Sandra Torres, a former Guatemalan first lady, of criminal association and accepting campaign funding from known drug traffickers. She denied the allegations. Mr. Giammattei won and took over as the new president of Guatemala in 2020.[14]

---

14. Sandra Cuffe, "Guatemala Elects Right-Wing President amid Dismal Turnout," *Washington Post*, August 12, 2019, https://www.washingtonpost.com.

3

A Christian Response

Catholics believe that our salvation is solely in the hands of God and cannot be earned, but that our actions, nevertheless, including how we respond to people like Gilberto, matter. Our guide is both Scripture and long-standing Catholic teaching. For Catholics, our goal is to form habits that lead us to become virtuous people who delight in God and in following God's law. We understand that, consistent with the natural law, first and most fully articulated by St. Thomas Aquinas, our selfish actions (for example, placing our own comfort over the safety of others) have consequences. Our selfish actions represent our choice to turn away from God and God's salvation—curling into ourselves. What does Scripture have to say about how we must treat migrants?

Hebrew Scriptures

The Bible portrays the periodic need to migrate as characteristic of being human. Both the Hebrew Scriptures and the New Testament speak consistently and coherently about the requirement to welcome the suffering stranger and treat the person with compassion. Indeed, the Hebrew Scriptures are the story of migration; humans migrate throughout the Scriptures both as a result of situations they themselves cause and situations caused by others. The story begins in the book of Genesis, with Adam and Eve, the first humans, whose actions cause them to be expelled from the Garden of Eden, their homeland (Gen 3:22–24). The first humans thus become the first migrants.

Their son Cain soon murders his younger brother, Abel, and, as his punishment, becomes a "wanderer on the earth," who eventually migrates to the land of Nod, "east of Eden" (Gen 4:12–16). Noah, a "righteous and blameless" man who "walked with God" (Gen 6:9), is directed by God to build an ark, fill it with a pair of every creature, and store up food to survive the ensuing flood. Noah and his household leave behind their home and everyone and everything they know, and eventually repopulate the earth as migrants.

Abram, who became Abraham—the father of Jews, Christians, and Muslims—lived the life of a migrant. Abram's father migrates with him from their native land of Ur of the Chaldeans to settle in Haran (Gen 11:31–32). But Abram hears God's call and takes his wife Sarai and nephew Lot, and all the possessions they have, to the land of Canaan. Here, Scripture tells us: "The Lord appeared to Abram and said: to your descendants I will give this land" (Gen 12:1–9). They resettle in Canaan as migrants.

But Abram, Sarai, and their extended group cannot survive on the land God gave them because of a severe famine. To save their lives, Abram and Sarai migrate again—to Egypt, where Abram does whatever it takes to survive in a foreign land: namely, he dishonestly passes off his beautiful wife as his sister, so that he will be allowed to stay with her in Egypt, and his own life won't be in jeopardy (Gen 12:10–16). Abram thrives in Egypt, grows rich, and, eventually, after his ruse is discovered, migrates with Sarai back to Canaan (Gen 13:7).

When they return, God gives the rechristened "Abraham" the land of Canaan forever (Gen 13:14–15). Migration appears to be at an end. But showing that the periodic need to migrate is part of the human condition, Abraham's descendants, due to another severe famine, are eventually unable to remain in Canaan again. Joseph, one of the sons of Jacob, had already been taken as a slave to Egypt, the victim of his brothers' jealousy. Joseph has become powerful and assimilated into the Egyptian pharaoh's household (cf. Gen 40–41). When the famine strikes Canaan, Jacob and his sons (Joseph's brothers) themselves migrate to Egypt (cf. Gen 41–46). The powerful Joseph ultimately welcomes to Egypt his father and the very brothers who mistreated him. Joseph ensures that they flourish as migrants.

After several centuries in Egypt, Jacob's descendants have multiplied and pose a threat to the Egyptians. The king oppresses and enslaves them (cf. Exod 1:8–11). The Book of Exodus recounts the Egyptians' mistreatment of the Israelites and God's help in orchestrating their escape, led by Moses. Exodus describes the escape and the ensuing forty years of wandering of the migratory Israelite people, roaming in the desert. These and many other stories in the Hebrew Scriptures show that, while the causes of migration are many, periodic migration is truly part of being human.

In the Mosaic Law, God commands (not suggests): "You shall not wrong or oppress a resident alien; for you were aliens in the land of Egypt" (Exod 22:21). God's command is repeated in the book of Leviticus: "The alien who resides with you shall be to you as the citizen among you; you shall love the alien as yourself, for you were aliens in the land of Egypt: I am the LORD your God" (19:33–34), and again in Deuteronomy: "You shall also love the stranger, for you were strangers in the land of Egypt" (10:18–19).

The command does not suggest that loving the stranger will be easy or that no sacrifices will be involved. Nevertheless, concern for the well-being of the suffering stranger is at the very core of the Mosaic Law.

Why are the Hebrew Scriptures so insistent on the gracious, fair, and welcoming treatment of migrants? There are at least two reasons: first, God's people must not replicate the nativist attitudes and oppressive treatment they experienced in Egypt—because those are not God's ways.

Second, God loves Israel, but God loves the sojourner too.[1] In Deuteronomy 10, God says:

> For the LORD your God is God of gods and the Lord of lords, the great God, mighty and awesome, who *is not partial* and

---

1. Daniel Carroll, "Biblical Perspectives on Migration: Contributions from the Old Testament," *Mission Studies* 30 (2013): 19.

takes no bribes, who executes justice for the orphan and the widow, and who *loves the strangers*, providing them food and clothing. *You shall also love the stranger*, for you were strangers in the land of Egypt. (Deut 10:17–19; emphasis added)

Many stories in the Bible, and the Mosaic Law itself, show God's way. They direct all people to emulate God's own nature.

The New Testament

What does Christ say about migration? Jesus began his public ministry at the synagogue in Nazareth, where he had been brought up. He stood there to read from the scroll of the prophet Isaiah:

He unrolled the scroll and found the place where it was written: "The Spirit of the Lord is upon me, because he has anointed me to bring good news to the poor. He has sent me to proclaim release to the captives and recovery of sight to the blind, to let the oppressed go free, to proclaim the year of the Lord's favor."

And he rolled up the scroll, gave it back to the attendant and sat down. The eyes of all in the synagogue were fixed on him. Then, he began to say to them, "Today, this scripture has been fulfilled in your hearing." (Luke 4:16–21)

Announcing his fulfillment of the Law, Jesus drew from the deep well of the Hebrew Scriptures and their repeated insistence that God's way consists of love for the oppressed, the poor, and the suffering stranger. Jesus says that we, as God's people, must love the oppressed, the poor, and the suffering stranger as God does. In contrast, Jesus never taught the importance of wealth acquisition, nation-states with ethnic or cultural unity, or closed borders.

One of the best places to see that Jesus absolutely requires that we, his followers, must welcome the suffering migrant stranger is his clarion call of God's final judgment in the Gospel of Matthew:

When the Son of Man comes in his glory, and all the angels with him, then he will sit on the throne of his glory. All the nations will be gathered before him, and he will separate people one from another as a shepherd separates the sheep from the goats, and he will put the sheep at his right hand and the goats at the left. Then, the king will say to those at his right hand, "*Come, you that are blessed by my Father, inherit the kingdom prepared for you from the foundation of the world*; for I was hungry and you gave me food, I was thirsty and you gave me something to drink, *I was a stranger and you welcomed me*, I was naked and you gave me clothing, I was sick and you took care of me, I was in prison and you visited me."

Then the righteous will answer him, "Lord, when was it that we saw you hungry and gave you food, or thirsty and gave you something to drink? *And when was it that we saw you a stranger and welcomed you*, or naked and gave you clothing? And when was it that we saw you sick or in prison and visited you?" And the king will answer them, "Truly I tell you, just as you did it to one of the least of these who are members of my family, you did it to me."

Then, he will say to those at his left hand, "You that are accursed, depart from me into the eternal fire prepared for the devil and his angels; for I was hungry and you gave me no food, I was thirsty and you gave me nothing to drink. *I was a stranger and you did not welcome me*, naked and you did not give me clothing, sick and in prison and you did not visit me."

Then, they will answer, "Lord, when was it that we saw you hungry or thirsty or a stranger or naked or sick or in prison, and did not take care of you?" Then, he will answer them, "*Truly I tell you, just as you did not do it to one of the least of these, you did not do it to me.*" *And these will go away into eternal punishment, but the righteous into eternal life*. (Matt 25:31–46; emphasis added)

In other words, Jesus says that we will eventually find ourselves on the right (with the sheep) or on the left (with the goats, who will go away into eternal punishment). He tells us plainly what we must do to be on the right side.

According to Matthew, how we respond to the suffering stranger at our country's border is not an armchair question. Jesus taught that the two greatest commandments are "You shall love the Lord your God with all your heart and with all your soul and with all your mind and with all your strength. The second is this: Love your neighbor as yourself. No other commandment is greater than these" (Mark 12:30–31; see also Matt 22:39; Luke 10:27). For those of us who think that by "neighbor," Jesus means only people who look like us or people we like or those who attend our church or already live in our neighborhood or share our culture, Matthew is clear: our final judgment will be based not on how we treat our friends but on our treatment of the stranger. The stakes could not be higher (cf. 25:31–46).

PART II

GABRIELA AND JAVIER

It is a high crime indeed to withdraw allegiance from God in order to please men, an act of consummate wickedness to break the laws of Jesus Christ, in order to yield obedience to earthly rulers, or under pretext of keeping the civil law, to ignore the rights of the Church; "we ought to obey God rather than men." (Acts 5:29)

—Pope Leo XIII, *Sapientiae Christianae*
(On Christian Citizens), January 10, 1890

4

Gabriela and Javi's Story

There are certain specific kinds of behavior that are always wrong to choose . . . choosing them is a moral evil.
—Pope John Paul II, *Veritatis Splendor,*
June 6, 1993

Gabriela was born to parents Ana and Javier in the city of Durango, in the state of Durango, Mexico, in 1999. Her brother, Javier Jr., called Javi, was born the next year. They came to the border by themselves, asking for help in 2015, when Gabriela was sixteen and Javi was fifteen years old.

Family Background

Their journey to the United States came after years of family violence, abuse, and, ultimately, abandonment. When Gabriela and Javi were young, their father worked at a welding company, sorting rods and generally helping out, and their mother sold cosmetics door-to-door. There was just enough money to keep the family afloat, but the children's lives were full of uncertainty. The father was an alcoholic who became violent when he drank. Even though the family had problems, Javi remembers being happy until about the age of ten. Gabriela and Javi regularly saw their father become enraged and irrational when drinking. He often beat their mother, Ana. One time, they saw Javier hit Ana so hard that he broke her ribs. She cowered on the floor. Javier also beat young Javi, sometimes with shoes and belts; other times kicking and punching him. Javier routinely belittled his son, calling him *hijo de la chingada* ("son of a whore"), *inútil* ("useless"), *pendejo* ("stupid"), and *wey* ("fool"). By the time Javi had reached fifth grade, he started to have problems at school. Other children bullied and made fun of him. Javi didn't understand why. He often fought with the bullies and was sent to the principal's office.

When Javi was thirteen, his father told him that it was time for him to support himself. Javi started working at a bakery. But Javier took the money he earned. As Javier's drinking worsened, the family's financial troubles became increasingly serious. They were evicted from their house and moved to a small apartment in a more dangerous neighborhood.

In 2013, when Gabriela was fifteen and Javi was fourteen, Ana fled her husband's abuse, moving to Los Angeles. Ana saw no alternative to leaving her children with their violent father, a decision that was quite painful for them. She got a small apartment and found work in a Mexican bakery. She sent money to Javier to support the children, but he rarely used it for them.

In Durango, Gabriela and Javi continued to attend school, but they had little support and no structure at home. Without Ana, Javier's mental situation deteriorated further. He drank even more often. Sometimes, Javier left home at night and didn't return until the next day. The children often did not know where he was, but they were relieved when he was gone.

Gabriela's and Javi's lives fell apart entirely on one particular day in the summer of 2015. Fourteen-year-old Javi stayed late at school. When he got home in the late afternoon, only his father was there. Javi noticed that Javier was shaky and acting strange, but he just tried to stay out of his way. As evening approached, Javier surprised Javi by giving him some money and telling him to go out and buy himself some dinner. This was highly unusual, and Javi didn't know what to make of it, but he was happy to have money and went to buy himself something to eat.

While Javi was gone, Gabriela returned home from school. Javier was drinking in the bedroom when she arrived. She turned on the television and sat down on the couch in the apartment's living room.

Around 7:30 that evening, Javier emerged and grunted that he was going out. He left without saying more but returned within thirty minutes. When Javier walked back in the door, Gabriela thought he seemed very nervous and somehow different. Javier went straight into the bedroom. Minutes later, he came out, completely naked. Gabriela was shocked. She froze in place, seated on the couch. She turned away from Javier, squeezed her hands together tightly and stared at the television. She had never seen her father this way. Javier approached her and sat on the couch right next to her. He had to hold onto the couch to keep from falling over. Javier looked at Gabriela in a way that she had never seen before. She felt both intimidated and desperate.

Javier told Gabriela to touch his intimate parts. She couldn't move or look at him. He became aggressive and physically forced her hand, which she clenched into a tight fist. Javier pried it open and forced her to touch him. Gabriela sobbed, but Javier was stronger. When he reached for her chest, she pushed him away very hard and he lost his balance. Javier picked himself up and violently punched the wall. While he was distracted, Gabriela grabbed her phone and ran out. It was raining that night, so she kicked off her house slippers and ran barefoot until she saw a taxi. She hailed it and asked the driver to take her to her maternal grandmother's house. She had the feeling that her father was following her, but she couldn't see him through the rain on the rear window of the taxi.

When Gabriela arrived at her grandma's house, she ran inside, sobbing. Her grandmother and some folks at her house asked what happened, and she told them what Javier had done. Moments later, Javier arrived in another taxi and began banging on the front door, yelling for Gabriela to come outside. Some men in the neighborhood yelled at Javier to leave, but Javier continued to pound on the door. One neighbor picked up a heavy pipe and approached Javier. They got into a fight, and the man hit Javier over the head with the pipe. Javier fell to the ground, bleeding.

While Gabriela was in the taxi, she called her mother, Ana, in Los Angeles who, in turn, called Javi. Ana told Javi only that he should go immediately to his grandmother's house. Javi didn't know what had happened, but with a feeling of dread, the young teen rode his bicycle to his grandma's house. When Javi got there, he saw his father lying on the ground outside, bloody and surrounded by angry men. Javi felt awful seeing Javier this way and was angry on his dad's behalf.

Some neighbors, hearing the noise of the fight, called the police. An ambulance pulled up, and Javi was surprised to see his father try to get up and run away. Then, he was shocked to see the neighbors physically restrain Javier. The police arrived, and Javi watched them manhandle his father into a police car and drive away. A bystander finally told Javi that his father had molested Gabriela. Javi was stunned and confused by his own competing feelings of anger on his father's behalf, rage at him, and revulsion at what the man had told him. Javi didn't know what to do, and no one paid any attention to him. He stood there until the crowd dispersed and then got on his bicycle and rode home alone.

Gabriela returned home from the police station the next day. Javi was the only one there. Neither Gabriela nor Javi ever returned to school. They existed on their own in a kind of gray world as the days rolled by. Their grandmother told them they couldn't move in with her. No other relatives took them in; no one had much money anyway. Although the police kept Javier in jail for a few days, they ultimately let him go. He wasn't prosecuted. When Javier was released from jail, he took his things and moved in with a girlfriend. He didn't support or even reach out to Gabriela and Javi. Ana called the children regularly from Los Angeles to check on them, and she sent money for food, but she did not return to Durango to care for them.

Javi had another problem as well. Just after his father's attack on Gabriela, Javi's friend Erick got in a fight with a member of a gang that was active in Durango. Javi was there at the fight and was beaten by the gang members in the melee. After that, Javi was afraid to go outside at all because he thought the gang members would associate him with his friend Erick. Having run out of options, in September 2015, Gabriela and Javi decided to try to find their mother in the United States.

The Journey to the United States

The city of Durango is located in the Mexican state of Durango, south of the state of Chihuahua, in the middle of the country. Durango is due south of Texas—quite a distance from Los Angeles. It is about 1,360 miles from the city of Durango to the San Ysidro port of entry into the United States, near San Diego, California— the crossing that is closest to Los Angeles, where Ana lived. Gabriela and Javi made their way there, taking buses and walking. The first time they approached the border crossing to ask for asylum, U.S. agents turned them back. Gabriela ended up in a detention center in Tijuana. The younger Javi was left on the streets. The two tried again another day, again turning themselves in to U.S. border agents at the official San Ysidro crossing. This time, they were separated and sent to two different ORR juvenile detention centers within the United States. Both children were eventually released to their mother, Ana, at the end of December 2015, on the condition that Ana would make sure they attended school and bring them to their hearings in immigration court, where DHS lawyers would argue that they should be deported to Mexico.

Gabriela and Javi enrolled in a public high school in East L.A. The studious Gabriela excelled in math, but she was shy in speaking English. Javi struggled to find his place in the large, big-city high school, but with his curiosity and aptitude for language, he was a quick study at English. An eagerness and a tiny optimism began to emerge in Javi that was never nourished in Durango.

The Road to Legal Status

Ana recognized that, without lawyers, her children would not be allowed to stay in the United States. She repeatedly called the list of charity agencies she had been given when the children were released from custody. Most of the agencies told her they were full. Eventually, the agency KIND agreed to find a pro bono lawyer for Gabriela. Another agency called Immigrant Defenders Law Center, founded in 2015 with financial support from the Episcopal Diocese of Los Angeles, agreed to find a lawyer for Javi. The two agencies referred the children to the same pro bono lawyer. Unlike Gilberto, these children had not been "persecuted" in their home country "because of their race, religion, national origin, political opinion or social group"—the only five categories on which a claim for asylum can be based. Their story was one of abuse, neglect, and abandonment by their own father.

Applying for Special Immigrant Juvenile Status

Gabriela and Javi learned—as Gilberto had learned before them—that the roads to legal status in the United States are few and exceptionally narrow. U.S. law is not full of loopholes. They learned that it is actually full of landmines. But expressing the will of the American people, Congress created a road for "abandoned, abused or neglected" children from other countries in 1990, when it amended the Immigration and Nationality Act of 1965 to create something called "Special Immigrant Juvenile Status" (SIJS).

Under this law, children who have come to the United States under the age of twenty-one (and who are unmarried) may apply to USCIS for SIJS. If they get SIJS, they may eventually apply for green cards and become citizens. Although SIJS can only be awarded by USCIS, Congress, in its wisdom, decided that USCIS—a federal administrative agency—does not possess the necessary expertise in juvenile and family matters to determine whether a child has been "abandoned, abused or neglected" or to decide what is in a child's "best interest." Congress decided that such family-centric, factual decisions *must be made by state court judges* who handle juvenile and family matters.

In Gabriela and Javi's cases, this meant that, before applying to USCIS for SIJS, they first had to file a lawsuit in the California state court system, asking a family court judge to order them into the legal and physical custody of their mother, and then make three factual findings about them: (1) that they were "abandoned, abused, or neglected" by a parent in their home country; (2) that reunification with that parent is not viable; and (3) that it is not in the children's "best interest" to be returned to their home country. If Gabriela and Javi could file a lawsuit and get such orders from a family court judge in California, they could then apply to USCIS for SIJS and eventually apply for green cards.

Children without lawyers simply do not possess the skills necessary to prepare and pursue lawsuits in court. Even for children who are lucky enough to find a pro bono lawyer, the SIJS process is complicated. The required "findings" are not easy to obtain. Some family court judges in this country are hostile to the process; others are not familiar with it. The definitions of what constitutes "abandonment, abuse, and neglect" differ from state to state. Furthermore, most children find it painful and embarrassing to discuss their experience of parental abandonment, neglect, and abuse with anyone, much less lawyers. Many children—even seriously abused ones—do not admit to themselves that they have been abused or neglected, or that a parent is not coming back. To obtain SIJS, they have no choice.

Gabriela and Javi started the process by writing their life stories in journals. In addition to their lawyer, they worked with a grandmotherly Spanish-speaking volunteer called Martha DeLira, who is part of a group of volunteers recruited by the Roman Catholic Archdiocese of Los Angeles and trained by KIND. (More about Martha later.) Over time, Martha became like a grandmother to the two children, mentoring them, attending their school events, inviting them to her home on holidays, and schooling them on ways to acclimate to American culture. She even coached them on how to get along with their mother. Gabriela, Javi, Martha, and the lawyer met many times to prepare their case.

Gabriela and Javi's state court case was filed in September 2016. First, they petitioned the Los Angeles Superior Court to waive the hundreds of dollars of court fees they otherwise would have to pay every time they filed a document in the court system. Next, they applied to have a guardian *ad litem* appointed for themselves during the court case, as required under California law. A guardian *ad litem* is a noncustodial guardian appointed to advise the court, from the perspective of the best interest of the child. Family courts in California will not hear a case involving children and their parents without a guardian *ad litem*—but the system does not provide one. An immigrant child who doesn't know anyone must still find someone to be their guardian *ad litem* before their SIJS case can proceed. Martha agreed to take on this volunteer role.

After a fee waiver and a guardian *ad litem* order were in place, Gabriela and Javi petitioned the court to recognize Ana as their mother and to award her physical and legal custody. To get such an order, their birth certificates and identity documents had to be translated into English, and all the papers they filed in court had to be served on the children's father in Durango, Mexico. He had to be persuaded to sign a paper (in English and Spanish) acknowledging that he received the papers, and that he did not contest the jurisdiction of the California court over his children or the award of custody to their mother. But Javier did not want to engage with Ana or his children at all, much less to sign any legal documents. Accomplishing "service" of documents in a foreign country and obtaining consent from an abusive parent are often serious challenges in SIJS cases. Fortunately, Ana persuaded Javier to sign the papers.

Finally, Gabriela and Javi petitioned the family court to review the evidence they presented and to make the factual findings that both children had been "abused, abandoned or neglected" by their father in Durango, that reunification with him was not viable, and that it was not in their best interest to be returned to Mexico. Each child provided their own sworn testimony in writing. They submitted translations of police and medical records and school records. The evidence about the abuse, neglect, and lack of basic parental care in Mexico contrasted with evidence of how the children were thriving in Los Angeles.

For the 2016–2017 school year, Gabriela was offered a full scholarship from a private donor to attend a Catholic all-girls college preparatory high school. She dived into the new school, working hard to learn English and make friends. Initially, Gabriela relied heavily on Google Translate. But a day came when she realized she didn't need it anymore. Javi continued at the public high school. He learned English quickly because, unlike many teenagers, he was willing to try to speak in English and learn from his mistakes. Javi dreamed of joining the police or army, but he also knew that to accomplish his goals, he had to graduate high school and obtain a green card. Meanwhile, Javi participated in ROTC.

At the same time that the children were pursuing their case in state court, they also had to appear before a different judge in federal immigration court, plead to the charges against them—like Gilberto did—and ask the immigration judge to give them time to complete the lengthy SIJS process in the family court. They went to periodic immigration court hearings to prove that their SIJS case was moving forward and that they were attending school.

In March 2017, the Los Angeles family court judge conducted an evidentiary hearing, after which she awarded sole custody of the two children to Ana and made the factual findings necessary for the two to apply to USCIS for SIJS. They promptly applied . . . and then they waited. When Congress delegated the task of making factual findings about children's eligibility for SIJS to state court judges, Congress decided that USCIS (lacking expertise in family matters) is not allowed to second-guess state court judges' decisions. Officers at USCIS are supposed to check to make sure that a state judge actually made all the required findings, but they are not allowed to reconsider them. Federal law states that USCIS shall approve or deny an SIJS application—a straightforward matter of making sure the application is in order—*within 180 days* of the application's receipt. The time limit is mandatory.

Since the beginning of 2017, however, USCIS has routinely ignored federal law, sitting on SIJS applications long after the 180-day deadline has passed. Moreover, USCIS now routinely demands that SIJS applicants provide the evidence the state court judges considered, so that USCIS employees can re-evaluate their decisions. This conduct by a federal agency violates U.S. law. During their long waits for approval of SIJS, children sit on tenterhooks, wondering about their futures. USCIS's violation of law began to occur around the same time that former attorney general Jeff Sessions began to rail against the SIJS process and falsely to portray SIJS applicants in the press as gang members and "wolves in sheep's clothing."[1]

---

1. Lauren Dezenski, "Sessions: Many Unaccompanied Minors Are 'Wolves in Sheep's Clothing,'" *Politico,* September 21, 2017; Josh Saul, "Sessions: Young Immigrants Are 'Wolves in Sheep Clothing,'" *Newsweek,* September 22, 2017.

USCIS took almost a year to consider Gabriela's and Javi's SIJS applications. While the applications were pending, USCIS demanded that the two provide information that the Los Angeles family court judge had already considered in their cases. The children faced a choice: they could point out to USCIS that it had no legal right to request that evidence—and likely have their SIJS applications denied, or they could comply with the unlawful demand and hope for the best. They provided summaries of the evidence. Happily, Gabriela's and Javi's SIJS applications were ultimately granted in February 2018. The immigration court cases against them were dismissed.

The Outcome

Gabriela and Javi applied for "lawful permanent resident" status and obtained their green cards in early 2019. Gabriela graduated from high school in May 2019, with Martha and Ana applauding madly in the audience. She was admitted to several colleges. Her highest grades were in math and science, and she is planning for a future in medicine or engineering.

Gabriela has grown from the shy and deeply wounded girl who asked for help at the border to a poised, kind, and confident bilingual young woman with much to give to her adopted country. Javi recently got a library card and earned his drivers permit. His English is fluent. He is wounded, but at the same time, he is resilient and has a friendliness and curiosity that bode well for his future. Javi still hopes to join the military or the police when he finishes high school. He is a bright, funny, and generous young man who recently helped a struggling, undocumented student in his high school to find a lawyer.

5

External Forces

Why couldn't Gabriela and Javi get help in their hometown, Durango, or in their own country? Why didn't some government social services agency there take them in? Such agencies do not exist in Mexico. The need for child protective services in Mexico is tremendous. Almost half of Mexico's population (estimated in 2019 to be 126 million) is under the age of twenty. Nevertheless, public agencies for the support and protection of children are highly inadequate, and children's needs and rights are routinely ignored.

Government Assistance

Wealth disparity in Mexico is great. Although Mexico is among the fourteen richest countries as calculated by gross domestic product, half of the population lives below the poverty line. Public schools for children in Mexico are in particularly dire straits: almost half have no access to sewerage; a third have no drinking water; and more than 12 percent have no bathrooms.[1] Education is compulsory only to the age of fourteen. The educational system in Mexico is ranked the worst out of all thirty-one members of the Organisation for Economic Cooperation and Development.[2]

---

1. Danyel Harrigan, "Wealth Inequality: On the Causes of Poverty in Mexico," The Borgen Project, July 27, 2017, https://borgenproject.org/causes-of-poverty-in-mexico.

2. "Children of Mexico, Realizing Children's Rights in Mexico," Humanium, https://www.humanium.org/en/mexico.

The Mexican government simply does not fund children's homes or orphanages for abandoned youth like Gabriela and Javi. There are some seven hundred privately funded youth shelters in the country, but they house only a small fraction of abandoned children and have been called "black holes for children." While Mexican law ostensibly requires that privately funded youth shelters be supervised and monitored by the government, in practice, this does not happen.

Only a small number of Mexico's abandoned and abused children can actually even be accommodated in the privately funded shelters. The *Red Latinoamericana de Acogimiento Familiar* (RELAF), a Latin American foster-care network, estimates that there are around 400,000 children without parents to care for them in Mexico. The private shelters house only 30,000 children and 100,000 children are completely homeless, surviving day-to-day, on the streets. The great majority of abandoned or abused Mexican children receive no assistance whatsoever.[3]

Shouldn't Gabriela and Javi have tried to find a place at one of these shelters anyway, even if it was hard to get in? They certainly would not have been safe there. In 2010, after a year-long investigation into children's institutions in Mexico, Disability Rights International reported that Mexican children in shelters experience widespread filth and squalor and a lack of medical care. Due to a lack of government oversight, children literally disappear from these places and may be subject to sex trafficking and forced labor.[4] Martin Perez, the director of the Mexican Network for the Rights of Children, explained:

> The state is 30 years behind in terms of guaranteeing the rights of children in public policies. The state has never supervised

---

3. Christopher Kolezynski, "Orphanages in Mexico and Human Rights," *Borgen Magazine*, September 5, 2014, https://www.borgenmagazine.com. See also RELAF, "Por el Derecho a Vivir en Familia y Communidad," https://www.relaf.org/index_engl.html.

4. Kolezynski, "Orphanages in Mexico and Human Rights"; Emilio Godoy, "Mexico's Orphanages—Black Holes for Children," Inter-Press Service News Agency, August 18, 2014, http://www.ipsnews.net.

these establishments; every once in a while something comes
to light and it remembers them and turns its attention to them
... and that leaves children in a vulnerable position. The shelters become a black hole.[5]

Illicit Drug Trafficking

There is another issue outside of Gabriela's and Javi's control, and
perhaps even their understanding, that made their lives in Durango
exceptionally fragile and difficult. These children have been deeply
affected by the seemingly unlimited American appetite for illicit
drugs, including heroin, synthetic opioids, cocaine, and synthetic
methamphetamine.

Drug addiction in the United States is known to be widespread,
affecting every socioeconomic class and region of the country. As of
December 2018, drug overdose became the leading cause of deaths
in the country. Drug deaths are at the highest level ever recorded in
the United States. Every year since 2011, deaths as a result of a drug
overdose have outnumbered deaths by guns, motor vehicles, suicide,
and homicide.[6] The vast majority of those who overdose on opioids
(80 percent) are non-Hispanic white Americans.[7]

Opioids are a class of drug originally derived from the opium
poppy plant, which can now be produced synthetically. Opioid
addiction, which includes prescription drugs, synthetic fentanyl,
and heroin, is at epidemic proportions in the United States. The use
of prescription opioid medications, like oxycodone, to treat non-
surgical chronic pain conditions gained popularity in the 1990s, as
pharmaceutical companies sold prescribing doctors on the drugs'
efficiency. Many prescription-drug users have turned to heroin, the
drugs' illegal, cheaper cousin and to synthetically produced fentanyl,

---

5. Godoy, "Mexico's Orphanages."
6. Paul E. Knierim, Statement of Deputy Chief of Operations, Office of
Global Enforcement, Drug Enforcement Administration, U.S. Department of
Justice, before the Subcommittee on Border Security and Immigration, U.S. Senate, December 12, 2018, https://www.justice.gov.
7. Knierim, Statement of Deputy Chief of Operations.

when their doctors have declined to prescribe opioids for pain in recent years. With American patients addicted to opioids but unable to get their prescriptions renewed, heroin use in this country has skyrocketed. The Council on Foreign Relations reports that the supply of heroin in the United States has soared since 2016, and its price is a third of what it cost in the 1990s.[8]

Most of the illegal heroin and synthetic fentanyl in the United States comes over the border through Mexico. While most of the heroin *in the world* comes from Afghanistan, only a tiny portion of that heroin finds its way to the United States. Instead, the heroin that comes into the United States is grown in Colombia and Mexico and driven through Mexico and into the United States in trucks and passenger vehicles. Most of the illicit synthetic fentanyl that comes into the country is manufactured in China and brought to the United States in the same way—through Mexico.[9] Other drugs are trafficked through Mexico as well, including marijuana, cocaine, and methamphetamine. According to the U.N. Office on Drugs and Crime, around 90 percent of the cocaine that finds its way into the United States comes from the Andes, through Mexico.[10]

Most of the drugs smuggled into the United States from Mexico enter through official ports of entry—the legal crossings controlled by U.S. Customs and Border Protection. Contrary to what some believe, only a small amount of drugs are walked over the border in isolated places. Traffickers actually hide or disguise large volumes of drugs in secret compartments in passenger vehicles, tractor-trailers, and, to a lesser extent, on buses and cargo trains. Fully 90 percent of the heroin, 88 percent of the cocaine, 87 percent of the methamphetamine, and 80 percent of the fentanyl that comes into the United States comes this way—through legal ports of entry.[11]

8. Claire Felter, "Backgrounder—The U.S. Opioid Epidemic," Council on Foreign Relations, January 17, 2019, https://www.cfr.org.

9. Felter, "The U.S. Opioid Epidemic."

10. Jonathan D. Rosen and Roberto Zepeda, *Organized Crime, Drug Trafficking and Violence in Mexico* (Lanham, MD: Lexington Books, 2016), 3.

11. Brianna Lee, Danielle Renwick, and Rocio Cara Labrador, "Back-

The effects of these drugs on the American public have been exhaustively reported. Less noticed has been the devastating effect of America's appetite for drugs on ordinary Mexicans like Gabriela and Javi, whose culture is saturated with the extreme violence that accompanies drug trafficking.

The Cartels

Corruption in Mexico has long run deep. Impunity levels for even the most violent crimes are astonishingly high. Criminals easily bribe police officers, judges, government officials, and politicians. Not surprisingly, ordinary Mexicans have little confidence in law enforcement, since one can never know if the police are working with or for organized crime.[12]

The Mexican public does have confidence, however, in the constant but unpredictable violence of the drug cartels that wreak havoc in Mexico as they bring illicit drugs to the American consumer. Since the 1980s, these cartels have grown, splintered, forged alliances, broken alliances, and gone to war with one another over territory and trade routes.[13] The cartels include the *Sinaloa Cartel*, formerly led by Joaquín "El Chapo" Guzmán, who now resides in a supermax prison in Colorado; the *Jalisco New Generation*, which split from the Sinaloa Cartel in 2010, is increasingly powerful and pervasive, and prides itself on an extraordinary willingness to engage in violence against both Mexican government authorities and other cartels; the *Juarez Cartel*, a long-standing rival of the Sinaloa Cartel; the *Gulf Cartel*, today somewhat weakened; *Los Zetas*, a paramilitary splinter group of the Gulf Cartel that was initially made up of former army special forces troops; and the *Beltran-Leyva Organization*, formed when the Beltran-Leyva brothers (both now dead) split from the Sinaloa Cartel in 2008.

---

grounder—Mexico's Drug War," Council on Foreign Relations, January 24, 2019, https://www.cfr.org.

12. Rosen and Zepeda, *Organized Crime*, 9.

13. Lee, Renwick, and Labrador, "Mexico's Drug War"; Knierim, Statement of Deputy Chief of Operations, 6–8.

New leaders and new groups are constantly emerging. The cartels' combined income is estimated to be tens of billions of dollars a year, entirely fueled by the American appetite.[14]

Drug production and trafficking in and through Mexico, which has existed for at least a hundred years, has been geographically concentrated in three Mexican states, colloquially known as the Golden Triangle—Sinaloa, Chihuahua, and Durango.[15] The cartels' effect on ordinary people who live in these places, like Gabriela and Javi, cannot be overstated. The threat of violence is always present. According to data collected by the leading Mexican newspaper *Reforma*, during the presidency of Felipe Calderón—from 2006 to 2012—49,253 Mexicans were executed by the drug cartels. This meant that twenty-one people were killed by the cartels every day of the Calderón administration. Of these so-called narco-executions, 4,645 of the bodies showed signs of torture, and 1,892 bodies were beheaded. Sixty percent of the drug-related murders in Mexico occurred in just five of its states, one of which was Durango.[16]

During the six-year Calderón government, thirty-two municipal presidents (mayors) in Mexico were executed by cartels. The state with the highest number of murdered mayors (five) was Durango.[17] During this same period, fourteen Mexican journalists were murdered and twelve more "disappeared," according to the Committee to Protect Journalists. Five of the journalists were in Durango.[18] This violence did not end when Mr. Calderón's term ended in 2012 and Enrique Peña Nieto took over. Nor has it ended under current president Andrés López Obrador, who took office in 2018. In fact, Mexican news outlet *Milenio* reported on July 1, 2019, that there were 2,249 murders in Mexico in June 2019 alone, the highest monthly total in twelve years. Stratfor, a security intelligence group that advises Fortune 500 companies and universities on Mexican

---

14. Ibid.
15. Ibid., 2.
16. Rosen and Zepeda, *Organized Crime*, 41–42.
17. Ibid., 48.
18. Ibid., 48–49.

cartel violence, observed that in 2019, Mexico was on its way to a new annual record for narco-murders:

> To those who closely follow violence in Mexico, the reports can sometimes seem overwhelming: Two shot dead in Cancun; 15 murdered in the last 24 hours in Tijuana; 12 dismembered bodies found in trash bins in Jalisco, etc. The headlines come in day after day in a steady rhythm of violence and the photos are worse than the headlines. Images of dismembered bodies or of *"narcomantas,"* messages from cartels on banners, left next to severed human heads, appear at least weekly.[19]

Children like Gabriela and Javi, from Durango, Mexico, live every day in this culture of violence. When they are abused or abandoned, they have no safety net. There is nowhere to turn when their parents fail them.

---

19. "Stratfor/Worldview, Murder in Mexico in 2019: A Midyear Checkup," Stratfor Assessments, July 11, 2019, https://worldview.stratfor.com.

6

The Catholic Way

How should Catholics think about—and act toward—children like Gabriela and Javi and the tens of thousands of other desperate children and families coming to the border asking for help? May a Catholic decide that these children are "someone else's problem," or just "too much," or that "migrants like these will take away opportunities from my children" and simply look away? May Catholics decide that Americans come first? May we conclude that America has enough problems with crime, homelessness, poverty, and hungry children in our own cities that must be fixed first before we welcome any strangers?

Faced with suffering people who are seeking to save their own lives, may Catholics ever weigh "the empirical costs and benefits of immigration"—as did a Catholic op-ed writer for *America* magazine in 2017—and on that basis, support closing the border to immigrants?[1] Is it true that church teaching supports border walls and that "it is a country's right and even its duty to say 'No' to some perfectly nice people" at the border?[2]

While there is no single Catholic moral response to *all* migration situations, when the "perfectly nice people" in question are suffering children and families who are running from life-and-death circumstances, the answer is no. Jesus *never* permits us to weigh the value of their lives against other existing difficulties, to turn our backs, or to

---

1. Pascal-Emmanuel Gobry, "I Am Catholic and Don't Know What I'm Supposed to Believe about Immigration," *America*, September 12, 2017.

2. Gobry, "I am Catholic."

send them away. Catholics may never do so, even if U.S. law allows precisely that response.

Revelation and Reason

There *is* a "Catholic way" of considering complicated moral issues, such as our response to the seemingly endless waves of suffering children and families asking for help at the border. Many Catholics have simply never learned it. This Catholic way doesn't choose between, for example, helping the homeless in this country *or* helping suffering migrants at the border. Catholics do both. The Catholic way does not value the life of a child from Nogales, Arizona, more than the life of a child from Nogales, Mexico. Catholics help both children. The Catholic way does not prioritize protecting an unborn child over a child asking for help at the border. The very same church teaching guides our responses to both children. *The Catholic way leads us to help all the suffering people in God's world, to the best of our ability, one by one, as they come before us.*

How does this work? Unlike Protestant traditions, Catholics do not turn only to Scripture, though the Word of God is certainly important. Nor do we pick through the Bible, as did Mr. Sessions, to find quotations that—in isolation—might seem to support our own ideas about how to address difficult problems. As Catholics, we rely on the two Rs: *revelation*, which includes both Scripture and the longstanding teaching of the church, and our God-given ability to *reason*.

Natural Law

For Catholics, the starting point for moral dilemmas has long been the concept of natural law, including its deep respect for God's creation, life. The idea of a natural law—unchanging moral principles that are the basis for all human conduct—appeared in Platonic, Stoic, and Aristotelian thought, several centuries before Christ. Natural law appears in early Christian writings, but Thomas Aquinas, in the thirteenth century, is generally seen as the master systematician of a natural law that is based on the creator God—

who created us in God's own image—and God's divine providence.[3] Aquinas's description of natural law, and his deep wrestling with all of its implications, underlies Catholic respect for life, including the teachings about what human life *is* and is *for*, that abortion of an unborn human is against God's will, and that Catholics care for suffering children in all circumstances, without exception.

Thomas Aquinas

What is natural law and how are we to comply with it? Aquinas taught that natural law is the part of God's eternal law that concerns humans on earth. He taught that natural law is unchanging, and that as humans we possess both the God-given ability to recognize natural law and the free will to comply with it—or not. Aquinas wrote that natural law is universal and written on every human heart. In simple terms, natural law is God's way for us. It is God's universal principles for how God's world works best and how we must act in it.[4]

Aquinas says that every human person has the capacity to grasp the universal first principles of natural law. The very first of these, upon which all the others are based, is that "good is to be promoted and evil is to be avoided."[5] But what does that really mean in a postmodern, relativistic world, where everyone argues that one's own ideas are good, and some contend that nothing is really evil? The second principle of natural law is that "whatever is a means of preserving human life and of warding off obstacles to life, belongs to the natural law."[6] Consistent with this deep reverence for life, Aquinas wrote that caring for and educating children, and whatever pertains

---

3. Thomas D. D'Andrea, "The Natural Law Theory of Thomas Aquinas," The Witherspoon Institute Online Center, *Natural Law, Natural Rights and American Constitutionalism*, 2011, http://www.nlnrac.org/classical/aquinas.

4. Anton C. Pegis, ed., *Introduction to St. Thomas Aquinas, Summa Theologiae Segunda Pars*, q. 94, Art. 4, 640–42; q. 94, Art. 5, 642–44; and q. 94. Art. 6, 644–45.

5. Ibid., q. 94, Art. 2, 635–38.

6. Ibid., 637.

to man's natural inclination to know the truth about God and to live in society, are the fundamentals of natural law.[7]

Thomas Aquinas taught that the purpose and ultimate end of every human is to know God and to share in God's divinity. He taught that the human "will"—that aspect of us that moves us to sin or not to sin—is actually an *appetite* that we control with our God-given intellect—our ability to reason. Aquinas saw that our intellect can, but often doesn't, direct our will to act in ways that lead to knowing God.[8] He saw that not only can we use reason to direct our wills to overcome our selfish appetites to sin, but we must try to do so.[9] Consequently, we actually participate in our salvation by trying—and trying again—to overcome our selfishness, and to live virtuously, in accord with natural law.

Catholics believe that while salvation is ultimately and solely in the hands of God and cannot be earned, our efforts to be virtuous here on earth do matter. Our ordinary daily actions—everything from losing our tempers, to harsh words, to ignoring another person's suffering, to offering a smile to a stranger—form *habits*. Our habits can become virtues—or they can form the opposite of virtues. Our selfish habits have real consequences for us because they truly represent our free choice to turn away from God. As Catholic Christians, our goal is to form habits that lead to being virtuous people who delight in God and in living in a way that is consistent with God's natural law.

Of course, it is not always easy to know how to comply with the first principle of natural law: to "promote good and avoid evil." On many daily matters, Catholics use one's reasoned judgment, nourished by the sacraments and prayer and informed by Scripture and church teaching. But are there some things that are always wrong for Catholics? Are there things that are in every case morally evil?

---

7. Ibid., 638.

8. Thomas Aquinas, *Summa Theologiae Prima Pars, Latin-English Edition* (Scotts Valley, CA: NovAntiqua, 2008), q. 80–81.

9. Ibid., q. 81, Art. 3, 2.

Are some things always a violation of natural law . . . a choice to turn away from God? For Catholics, the answer is, yes.

Pope John Paul II

Oxford professor of law and legal philosophy John Finnis, a Catholic, wrote on this in 1991. Quoting Pope St. John Paul II in explaining that "exception-less" moral norms ("acts which *per se* and in themselves, independent of circumstances, are always seriously wrong by reason of their object") are the constant teaching of the Catholic tradition, and are binding on all Catholics.[10] Finnis wrote that although these options are "logically possible and readily conceivable," in the way that abortion and euthanasia are possible and readily conceivable, they are always morally wrong for Catholics, regardless of the circumstances. The church has always taught that these "moral absolutes" are and will always be wrong, regardless of the particular circumstances or difficulty of the situation.

John Paul II's 1993 encyclical *Veritatis Splendor* reiterated that moral absolutes absolutely exist—"certain specific kinds of behavior that are always wrong to choose." John Paul II taught that choosing these specific behaviors always involves a "moral evil," and that Catholics may never choose a moral evil, even with good intentions or a belief that some other good will ultimately come of it.[11] John Paul II proclaimed that Catholics *must* follow papal authority on these matters, and he soundly rejected the exercise of individual "prudential judgment" when a moral absolute is involved. John Paul II wrote that relativistic thinking—weighing some lives against others—rejects the church's natural law assumptions about what a human is, what sin is, what the meaning and purpose of human life are, what is the way to true happiness, and who God is.

In *Veritatis Splendor*, John Paul II left no doubt as to what acts are always off-limits for Catholics in moral decision making. Quoting Romans 3:8, he wrote, "there are those who say: And why not do

---

10. John Finnis, *Moral Absolutes, Tradition, Revision and Truth* (Washington, DC: Catholic University Press, 1991).

11. John Paul II, *Veritatis Splendor*, June 6, 1993, no. 78, http://w2.vatican.va.

evil that good may come? Their condemnation is just."[12] He confirmed that no step in a Catholic's plan of action may involve formal cooperation with evil.[13] John Paul II provided a list of "acts which, *per se* and in themselves, independent of circumstances, are always seriously wrong":

> *Whatever is hostile to life itself,* such as any kind of *homicide, genocide, abortion, euthanasia and voluntary suicide*; whatever *violates the integrity of the human person,* such as mutilation, physical and mental torture and attempts to coerce the spirit, whatever *is offensive to human dignity, such as subhuman living conditions, arbitrary imprisonment, deportation, slavery, prostitution and trafficking in women and children*; degrading conditions of work which treat laborers as mere instruments of profit, and not as free responsible persons; all these and the like are a disgrace.[14]

John Paul II's teaching, based on God's unchanging natural law, makes clear how Catholics must respond to particular migration situations we encounter. Catholics may never engage in, intend, work for, or cooperate with the things John Paul II identified that are hostile to life itself. Catholics may never support those whose conduct or strategy is offensive to human dignity, such as putting migrating human beings in subhuman living situations, imprisonment of children or, when lives are at stake, deportation. Such things are, in John Paul II's words, "a disgrace."

In contrast, abortion and the deportation of suffering children and families in life-threatening situations are entirely legal under U.S. law. The United States is currently holding tens of thousands of noncriminal asylum seekers in subhuman, for-profit prisons. This

---

12. *Veritatis Splendor*, no. 78.

13. "Formal" cooperation is a concept that recognizes that Catholics have to cooperate with people with whom they disagree to live in society. "Formal cooperation" refers to situations where the Catholic explicitly or tacitly *intends* (agrees with or desires) the moral wrong.

14. *Veritatis Splendor*, no. 80 (emphasis added).

country regularly turns away suffering and persecuted people to the very places from which they fled. The U.S. Supreme Court, on which sit five Catholics, upheld a Trump administration policy permitting border agents to turn away asylum seekers who did not ask for asylum in the dangerous countries they passed through on the way to the U.S. border. Even before this ruling, terrified men, women, and children seeking help were routinely turned away or have been languishing in detention centers, where they live without the most basic necessities of life, including soap, a toothbrush, or a place to sleep.[15] Catholics may never support or cooperate with these practices. They may not cooperate with or avert their eyes from this conduct in the hope that some other perceived good may come.

As John Paul II explained, natural law requires that, when a child asks for protection, support, or to be reunited with family, we must always respond with love. We may never reject the child, turn our backs, or send the child to a dangerous place as someone else's problem. We may never weigh this child's well-being against some other societal problem. *Catholics aid the human person in front of us.*

Natural Law versus a Human Law

United States' law, however, permits, and routinely engages in, all of these practices.[16] For example, unless children can meet the stringent standards of asylum (as did Gilberto) or can find a lawyer to help them obtain Special Immigrant Juvenile Status by winning a lawsuit in state court and then navigating the requirements of USCIS (as did Gabriela and Javi), this country routinely holds them in detention facilities and deports them to the places from which they fled.

---

15. See, e.g., Meagan Flynn, "Detained Migrant Children Got No Toothbrush, No Soap, No Sleep. It's No Problem, Government Argues," *Washington Post*, June 21, 2019, https://www.washingtonpost.com. The government lawyer who made this argument on behalf of the Trump administration is featured in the story of the Flores family in chap. 9.

16. U.S. law is, in Thomas Aquinas's terms, "human law." Human law is not inviolable, nor is it ever the highest law for Christians. When human law is unjust, it is "no law at all."

As Christians—indeed as human beings—we may never support those who engage in prohibited moral absolutes like turning their backs on a child. We may never condone discarding a human life, even in the hope that some other desired end may come, for example, the purported well-being of our own children, protecting our riches, the flourishing of our economy, or the appointment of judges who are anticipated to take action on other issues. For Catholics, it is never permissible to cooperate with evil. Our own salvation is at stake.

As Thomas Aquinas taught, turning our backs on the suffering of others forms habits that lead us away from God. Catholics know that we cannot save ourselves, but we are entirely free to turn away from God's salvation. We cannot cooperate with evil without turning away from God. This is why every step of our plans, including the ends and the means, must exclude evil.[17] Catholics may never weigh some human lives on one side against other lives, or perceived good, on the other.

The "Common Good"

What about Aquinas's concept of seeking the "common good"? Doesn't that mean that Catholics may choose whatever strategy leads to the greatest good for the greatest number of people? Quite simply, no, it doesn't. The "greatest good for the greatest number" is Jeremy Bentham's and John Stuart Mill's concept of "utilitarianism." Utilitarianism embraces the notion that some people may lose out entirely, but more people will thrive. The Catholic concept of the common good is not utilitarianism.

The Catholic concept of the common good is completely different. It comes from the natural law's recognition that humans are social creatures. Aquinas recognized that our human need to live in society with other people is intrinsic to our God-given human nature, and thus part of natural law. But Aquinas also saw that

---

17. Finnis, *Moral Absolutes*, 59–70, explains how, in Thomas Aquinas's moral reasoning, it is never permissible to cooperate with evil—every step of one's intended action, including the ends *and the means,* must exclude evil.

living in societies necessitates that we have human laws—created by humans in specific times and situations—for the common good of all people.[18] Human law for the common good is understood to mean laws that form a social order that enable *all* the people in the world (not some or even most of them) to find their way to God. It means a social order that helps *all* people to pursue and have the possibility of knowing and loving God, while living in society together. Everyone is included in the common good. Therefore, the common good cannot be determined by a popular vote, and it isn't what is best for me, my family, my town, my country, or my people. The common good doesn't permit some people to be left out entirely, as long as others, or even most people, get what they want. The Catholic concept of the common good certainly is not aimed at maximizing anyone's acquisition of money, consumer goods or property, or at protecting a standard of living for a particular group or nation. The Catholic common good does not recognize Americans as "exceptional" or "America first."

Saint Thomas Aquinas, and St. Augustine before him, taught that because human laws are created by fallible people, they are, from time to time, wrong. This is because our human judgment and perspective are always limited. As St. Paul noted, "we see in a mirror, dimly" (1 Cor 23:12). We often cannot see in real time that laws are unjust, and we frequently misunderstand consequences. Thomas and Augustine concluded that when a particular human law is not derived from natural law and for the common good, that law is not just, and it is no law at all.[19]

Unjust laws, like those enforcing slavery and then segregation in this country, and those that led to the Holocaust in Europe, never have a moral force on Catholics. We must ignore them. Of course, this doesn't mean that followers of Jesus who stand up to unjust laws won't experience consequences when they disregard unjust human laws. Christians who defied slavery and segregation laws in the United States, and people like Dietrich Bonhoeffer and Maximilian

---

18. Pegis, *Introduction*, q. 95, Art. 1.
19. Ibid., q. 95, Art. 2.

Kolbe, who defied Nazi laws in Germany, in fact, suffered terrible consequences. Today, we regard them as Christian martyrs and saints. Regardless of the consequences we may suffer for defying them, however, laws that allow desperate, suffering children and families to be jailed and deported to dangerous places are "no law at all." Catholics cannot defend them, and Catholics may not quietly tolerate them—as did many in Nazi Germany—even in the hope that some other good will come.

PART III

LILIANA AND THE FLORES FAMILY

The right of people to migrate is found in the natural law. It is inevitable, given the nature of the earth, which is vast and includes both habitable and uninhabitable places, that some families will migrate. The right of a family to be together in a living space is fundamental to natural law.

—Pope Pius XII,
Exsul Familia Nazarethana, August 1, 1952

Catholics must always protect the family as the "sanctuary of life"; our natural human rights include "the right to live in a united family and in a moral environment conducive to the growth of the child's personality."

—Pope St. John Paul II,
Centesimus Annus, 1991

7

Liliana's Story

Liliana Aguilar was born in December 2001 in the department (roughly equivalent to a state) of Copan, in the western part of Honduras. The town in which she lived, Santa Rosa, is the capital of the department and, with a population of approximately forty thousand, is the largest town in Copan. Most people who live there are very poor.

Family Background

Liliana is petite and pretty. She has a fierce intelligence and a strong will. Growing up, Liliana never knew her father, Armando, but she yearned to know him. Armando abandoned Liliana and her mother, Felicita, when Liliana was just two years old. Armando cut off contact with Felicita. He left Honduras and never supported them financially. Felicita never completed high school. She had no real skills and very few ways to support herself and her small daughter. Felicita subsisted with help from her own mother and from the various men she dated.

Liliana started school at a little kindergarten when she was five years old. Around this same time, Felicita became involved with a man called Emilio. She met Emilio through her mother, who had married and moved in with Emilio's father. With Emilio, Felicita hoped she had found security for herself and her young daughter. Felicita and the young Liliana moved into a one-room apartment with Emilio in Santa Rosa. Their lives there were very basic, with no bathroom or kitchen in their apartment.

Emilio supported the three as a well digger, but he was also a chronic alcoholic, who often used drugs. Young Liliana watched Emilio come home day after day, drunk and mean. She often saw him insult and abuse her mother. But Liliana was a tiny girl. She couldn't say or do anything about the way Emilio acted. Felicita often scolded Liliana to stay out of Emilio's way. Whenever Emilio would run out of money, the three moved to another place. Sometimes, they moved in with the grandparents. Felicita had three more children with Emilio.

After a year in kindergarten, Liliana attended a local primary school for the next six years. As was customary in her town, school started at 6:20 am and ended at 12:30 pm. Liliana easily made friends there and walked with them to and from school. Her teachers recognized her intelligence and abilities, and school became a haven for her. Life at home, however, was not easy. Emilio was a drunk and a bully. Many times, he spent all the money he had earned on alcohol and drugs, leaving Felicita with nothing to buy food for the children. Sometimes, Felicita sent young Liliana to find Emilio in the local bars at night and to beg him for money to buy food for the other children.

Liliana completed primary school at the end of 2012 at age eleven. She started working full time at a little restaurant in town called "La Fonda." She had goals for herself and wanted to attend high school, but Felicita could not pay. Liliana couldn't attend high school unless she got a job. Once she had a job, Liliana bought her own food and clothes, and paid her own school fees. She enrolled at a secondary school called Institute Carlos Castro in 2013. Again, she attended classes from 6:20 am to 12:30 pm and then went straight to La Fonda, where she worked until 9 pm. After paying her own expenses, Liliana gave the rest of her money to Felicita to support the younger children.

Emilio continued to abuse Felicita, but now, Liliana often found herself in the middle. As she entered her teen years, the petite girl began to talk back to the man who dominated her home and abused her mother. Felicita did not appreciate Liliana's interventions. She was terrified of losing Emilio. Felicita consistently defended her abusive partner to Liliana and criticized Liliana for talking back to him. Still, Liliana and Emilio argued all the time. Liliana repeatedly begged Felicita to kick Emilio out, but her mother always took Emilio's side. Felicita told Liliana to keep quiet, to stop causing trouble, and that as a man, Emilio was entitled to hit her if he chose to. Liliana told herself that she had to be strong and fearless because if she didn't, Emilio would beat her as well.

From about the age of twelve, Liliana grew increasingly curious about her birth father, Armando. She persuaded Felicita to ask Armando's parents for his phone number. Liliana tried to call Armando every six months or so. She learned that he was in the United States. Sometimes, Armando answered the phone, and twice, he sent her a little gift. But Armando never initiated a call to Liliana. He remained a mystery, though Liliana imagined that he was kinder and more handsome and successful than Emilio.

Conflict

When Liliana was fifteen, the family's landlord at the time told them to leave because of the fighting and loud arguments. Liliana reached out to Armando to help, repeatedly calling his phone number and sending texts. He didn't respond. When the family was evicted, they moved into a shed behind the grandparents' house. Inside, the shed was partitioned into two rooms, but only one of the rooms had a window, which was covered with cardboard. The shed had no plumbing or heat. The family of six slept in the room with the cardboard window. Emilio continued to drink and do his drugs, working only sporadically. One morning not long after they moved in, Liliana woke up to a particularly loud argument between Emilio and Felicita in the room without a window. Liliana got up fast and ran into the dark room. A drunken Emilio was waving a machete at Felicita. Liliana yelled at Emilio and ran to stand in front of her mother, between Felicita and Emilio's machete. Felicita tried to push Liliana behind her. Liliana shouted at Emilio and they argued. When Emilio lost his balance and fell to the floor, swearing and cursing, Liliana pulled Felicita out of the room. Once again,

Felicita was not grateful. She was enraged. Felicita still refused to leave Emilio or ask for outside help.

The Journey to the United States

This fight woke up something in Liliana. She knew that she could not continue to bluster her way through a life that involved Emilio. She realized that she would never be safe living with him and that her mother would not protect her. Liliana stuffed her few possessions into her backpack and left. She briefly stayed in town with Armando's parents, but they were both confined to wheelchairs and did not offer her a long-term home. Liliana decided to find Armando in the United States. She dreamed he would be the father she needed. Liliana left Copan, Honduras—the only place she had ever lived—on her own, at age fifteen. She had no one to protect her or to pay a *coyote* to guide her on the journey. She took what money she had from her job and made her way through Honduras, Guatemala, and Mexico by bus and on foot, stopping at migrant shelters and surviving on the generosity of strangers.

While Liliana was on her dangerous journey north, her mother, Felicita, was badly injured, ironically not by Emilio but by a herd of cattle on the road by the grandparents' house. Felicita's three-year-old son had wandered outside by himself. When Felicita realized he was gone, she caught sight of him on the road, with the herd trotting toward him. Felicita shouted to the little boy to run to a neighbor's house, but he froze in place. Felicita ran to him and fell on top of the little boy covering him while the cows trampled her. A bull's horn pierced her skull. Felicita recovered in the hospital but is now disabled. She can't remember even simple things.

The journey from Copan to Hidalgo, Texas, where Liliana approached the U.S. border crossing, was about 1,400 miles. She arrived in late November 2017. Customs and Border Protection agents sent Liliana to an ORR juvenile detention center called Southwest Key Antigua, in Benito, Texas. This facility was one of many run by a private company, under contract to the government. Although the Southwest Key organization calls itself a nonprofit, its president, Juan Sanchez, earned $3.6 million in 2017. Juvenile detention work is lucrative; in 2019, Southwest Key had an annual contract of $460 million to house migrant children and had collected more than $1 billion from the federal government since 2014.[1]

Liliana lived at the detention center with about two hundred other children for two months. In the meantime, the officials found Armando in Los Angeles, and he agreed to take custody of her, while she went through removal proceedings in immigration court. As with all the children who come to the border, Liliana would face lawyers from DHS in immigration court who would seek to persuade a judge to deport Liliana to Honduras. She would have to appear in court by herself, unless she could find a pro bono lawyer.

Broken Dreams

Armando signed a "Sponsor Care Agreement" with the Department of Health and Human Services, in which he promised to enroll Liliana in school, take care of her in his home, and accompany her to all of her immigration court hearings. Liliana was thrilled to leave the detention center in Texas and finally meet her father, Armando, in Los Angeles. But things did not turn out as she had dreamed they would. When she arrived in Los Angeles, Armando immediately drove her to an apartment where a woman called Isabel and her sister, Claudia, lived with three young girls who were Claudia's young daughters. Armando told Liliana that Isabel was his wife, but he did not live with her. He told Liliana that she would live with Isabel, Claudia, and the girls—all strangers to her. She realized that she did not know Armando either. She finally started to realize that Armando's biological tie to her did not make him her father.

Claudia told Liliana that her young daughters did not like Armando, so he was not allowed to come to the apartment. Liliana initially thought this was strange, but everything about her situation

---

1. Mark Berman, "Six Officials at Nonprofit Southwest Key, Which Runs Migrant Child Shelters, Earned More Than $1 Million in 2017," *Washington Post*, July 16, 2019, http://www.washingtonpost.com.

was strange. She assumed that Claudia's rule explained why she never saw Armando. The women did not allow Liliana to leave the apartment. Her contact with Armando was on the phone. She called him repeatedly about her situation, and, eventually, she began to argue with him.

Armando finally admitted to Liliana that he had been surprised by the call from a government official asking him to take custody of her. He had not wanted to agree but felt he could not refuse. Armando told Liliana that he was making arrangements for her to go back to Honduras. He repeatedly called Liliana's mother, Felicita, in Copan, demanding that Felicita's parents sell their home to buy a plane ticket for Liliana to return to Honduras.

Before Armando could arrange to have Liliana sent back to Honduras, she was removed from Isabel and Claudia's apartment by the Los Angeles Department of Children and Family Services (DCFS). That agency had received a tip about abuse in Isabel and Claudia's apartment. They investigated and concluded that Liliana was being abused by Armando and the women. DCFS assigned a social worker to Liliana and removed her from the home. Liliana was sent to live with Armando's sister, her Aunt Marta, who also lived in Los Angeles.

Current Situation

Liliana now lives with Aunt Marta and Marta's children. She finally feels safe. She is not afraid of being hurt by Emilio, and she does not have to work to be able to eat or attend school. She is seeing a counselor to deal with the trauma she has experienced in her short life and to talk about her feelings about Emilio and Armando. Liliana attends a magnet public high school in Los Angeles that has a special focus on visual arts and humanities where she is excelling. Liliana's favorite subjects are history and math, and her teachers rave about her work ethic and dedication to excellence. Liliana's Aunt Marta is helping her to adjust to her new situation. Liliana hopes to remain in Los Angeles and—maybe not surprisingly—wants to use her skills to become a lawyer.

Nevertheless, the immigration court proceedings loomed over Liliana. Aunt Marta initially tried to file a guardianship case in the Los Angeles Superior Court by herself, but she did not know how to do so. KIND finally found a pro bono lawyer for Liliana. They filed a case in state court, asking a judge to appoint Marta to be Liliana's legal guardian and officially to assign Liliana into her care. They presented the judge with extensive evidence of the "abandonment, abuse and neglect" that Liliana had suffered at the hands of her father, and proved both that it was not viable for Liliana to be reunited with him or her mother, and that it is not in her best interest to be sent back to Honduras, where there is no one to take care of her. Liliana applied to USCIS for SIJS status in January 2019. USCIS approved Liliana's petition in September 2019. While Liliana waits for her turn to apply for a green card, her case in immigration court continues, and she regularly checks in with the judge.

8

The Background

Liliana's life in Honduras was bleak, but did she really have to leave her country to survive? Why wasn't she cared for by her own community or her own government? Why is life so difficult for so many ordinary people in Honduras that they leave everything they have and know behind? Are Catholics in the United States justified in telling desperate Hondurans to "go back to where you came from" when their lives are at stake? Has the United States played any role in creating the situation faced by Hondurans in their own country today? To answer these questions, it is necessary to understand something about Honduras and its history.

Honduras is a small country of about nine million people (in contrast, the population of L.A. County is ten million).[1] Honduras is arguably the poorest country in Latin America. Currently, life is terribly difficult for most Hondurans. Crime and corruption have overwhelmed the police and judicial system. There is no working government social welfare system for children. In 2017, the rate of homicides in the entire world was 6.1 per 100,000 people. In the small country of Honduras, the number was 41.7 per 100,000 people. Only six countries in the world had homicide rates higher than 40 per 100,000 that year. In 2017, even with gun violence in the United States, the homicide rate for North America (including the

---

1. Peter J. Meyer, "Honduras: Background and U.S. Relations," *Congressional Research Service Report for Members and Committees of Congress*, updated June 4, 2019, 1; "Los Angeles County California Population 2019," World Population Review, http://www.worldpopulationreview.com.

United States and Canada) was 4.2 per 100,000 people.[2] In Honduras, not only is murder a common event, but almost 95 percent of homicides go unsolved. There, murder truly is an evil without consequences.[3]

Honduras is at the bottom of all the countries in Central America in per capita income, literacy, health care, life expectancy, and nutrition.[4] Unemployment is exceptionally high. In 2018, nearly 20 percent of Hondurans were unemployed or underemployed, and another 49 percent worked full time for less than the country's minimum wage, which amounts to about $2,500 per year.[5] More than 67 percent of Hondurans live below the poverty line, surviving on less than $3.20 per day.[6] In rural areas, nearly 63 percent of the Honduran population lives in "extreme poverty," are unable to satisfy basic nutritional needs, and are living on less than $1.90 per day.[7]

The education system in Honduras is rudimentary. Half of all children have left school by age twelve. Only one in four attends high school, usually because they are put to work to support their families.[8] Violence against women and children, often within families, is pervasive. Children are ten times more likely to be murdered in Honduras than in the United States. UNICEF reports that between 2008 and 2015, one Honduran child died a violent death every twenty-two hours.[9] Experts testify that, under the prevailing

---

2. United Nations Office on Drugs and Crime, *Global Study on Homicide* (Vienna: U.N. Office on Drugs and Crime, 2019), booklet 2, 26–29.

3. Roger A. Carvajal, "Violence in Honduras: An Analysis of the Failure in Public Security and the State's Response to Criminality," U.S. Naval Postgraduate School (June 2014).

4. Carvajal, "Violence in Honduras," 5.

5. Meyer, "Honduras," 8; "Country Reports on Human Rights Practices for 2015," U.S. Department of State, Bureau of Democracy, Human Rights and Labor (2015), https://www.state.gov.

6. Marc Silver and Malaka Gharib, "What's the Meaning of the World Bank's New Poverty Lines?" NPR, October 25, 2017, https://www.npr.org.

7. Meyer, "Honduras," 8.

8. Maria Verza, "In Honduras, Poverty and Gangs Help Drive Migration," *Seattle Times,* October 23, 2018, https://www.seattletimes.com.

9. UNICEF, *UNICEF Annual Report 2017: Honduras* (June 2018), https://www.unicef.org.

cultural norms, violence against children is not even regarded as wrong in Honduras. Indeed, children are not perceived to be persons with their own rights but instead are the possessions of their fathers. Due to their inferior societal status, children often experience hitting, kicking, burning with hotplates, humiliation, insults, inappropriate touching, and molestation *in the home.*

Causes of Poverty and Violence

At least three factors have been identified as contributing to the pervasive poverty, extreme violence, and almost total lack of justice in Honduras. First, law enforcement and the military are deeply corrupt. Second, the same street gangs that invaded Guatemala in the late 1980s and 1990s, including Mara Salvatrucha and Mara 18, invaded Honduras and now operate with near impunity. These gangs deal drugs, extort ordinary people, and murder their perceived enemies and others at random. They are responsible for a substantial percentage of homicides and much of the crime that affects citizens on a day-to-day basis.[10] Finally, Honduras is geographically located in a significant drug-trafficking corridor, between cocaine-producing countries in South America and the major consumer market for these drugs in the United States. According to the U.S. Department of State, the percentage of cocaine that comes into the United States through this corridor rose from 1 percent to 95 percent in the three years between 2007 and 2010.[11] The Congressional Research Service reports that today, heavily armed and well-financed transnational criminal organizations—cartels that traffic in both drugs and people—routinely battle one another over territory and routes in Honduras, buying and intimidating local institutions. Moreover, these criminal cartels have strong ties to

---

10. Meyer, "Honduras," 8; Steven Dudley, Elyssa Pachico, and Juan Jose Martinez, "Gangs in Honduras," Insight Crime, November 20, 2015, www.insightcrime.org.

11. Carvajal, "Violence in Honduras," 12, citing Nigel Inkster and Virginia Comolli, *Drugs, Insecurity and Failed States: The Problems of Prohibition* (New York: Routledge, 2012), 98.

Honduran politicians, who rely on illicit money to fund their election campaigns and lifestyles.[12]

Honduras's political leadership was corrupt long before the arrival of the cartels, but the corruption continues unabated. The current Honduran president, Juan Orlando Hernández, who came to power following a 2009 coup, obtained an unlawful second term in 2017 that was expressly prohibited by the Honduran constitution. He did this by replacing four sitting Supreme Court justices with new men who promptly approved his second term. The U.S. Congressional Research Service observed that the 2017 presidential election was also flawed by after-the-fact "updating" of vote totals, which handed the victory to Mr. Hernández, the incumbent.[13] Although the move was widely seen in Honduras as illegal and a violation of the independence of the Honduran judiciary, nothing was ever done about it. Mr. Hernández remains in office.

Doctors Without Borders has reported that following the 2017 election, Mr. Hernández's crackdown on protesters resulted in the death of twenty-two civilians and one police officer, and more than 1,300 detentions.[14] In September 2017, the son of former President Porfirio Lobo (in office 2010–2014) was sentenced in federal court in New York to twenty-four years in federal prison for conspiracy to import cocaine into the United States. Then, in November 2018, the U.S. Department of Justice charged current President Hernández's brother (himself a former member of Congress) with large-scale drug trafficking.[15] Additionally, although no charges have yet been brought, Mr. Hernández himself was a recent target of a Drug Enforcement Administration investigation.[16]

---

12. Meyer, "Honduras," 8.

13. Mark P. Sullivan et al., "Congressional Research Service, Latin America and the Caribbean: Issues in the 115th Congress," Homeland Security Digital Library (Washington, DC: Library of Congress, January 22, 2019), http://www.hsdl.org.

14. Doctors Without Borders, *Part 1: Cycles of Violence in Honduras* (October 16, 2018), https://www.doctorswithoutborders.org.

15. Meyer, "Honduras," 8–9, 20.

16. Meyer, "Honduras," 20.

American Involvement

Has the United States played any role in making Honduras the dangerous and corrupt place that it is today? Has our country participated in creating the desperate situation now faced by ordinary Hondurans? The answer is that the United States has been deeply involved in Honduran affairs for more than one hundred years.

Honduras has always been less developed than other Central American countries. The Mayans, whose civilization covered much of Mexico and Guatemala, once had a sophisticated city of twenty square kilometers in Copan, the department in which Liliana lived. But the Mayans had abandoned their city to the jungle long before Christopher Columbus arrived in 1502. When Columbus first came to what now constitutes Honduras, he encountered a variety of culturally and linguistically distinct native peoples. Spain gained control of the area in the 1540s, and the diseases that Spanish colonists brought with them largely wiped out the native populations. In the later part of the sixteenth century, migrants from other parts of Central America who were attracted by mining opportunities moved into the area. By the eighteenth century, subsistence farming had become the main way of life.[17]

Honduras won independence from Spain in 1823 as part of the Central American Federation—an alliance of what are now Nicaragua, Costa Rica, El Salvador, Guatemala, and Honduras. That alliance broke up in 1839, and Honduras then became an independent republic. In the other new republics, coffee soon emerged as an export crop that advanced their economies. An upper class of landowning coffee elites emerged. But coffee didn't take off in Honduras, which remained a backward country with poor (or no) infrastructure, deeply in debt (to the British), and led by a never-ending series of corrupt leaders. Into this environment, the American fruit businesses, backed by the U.S. military, arrived and bought influence at the turn of the twentieth century.

---

17. Richard Lapper and James Painter, *Honduras: State for Sale* (London: Latin America Bureau, 1985), 17–18.

The American Banana Companies

The American fruit companies were drawn to the northern coastal region of Honduras, where bananas grew well. Honduran leadership welcomed the Americans with open arms. They gave these fruit companies (Standard Fruit, United Fruit, and their predecessors) huge financial concessions, including mineral and other rights over land, exemption from paying customs duties and taxes, and the right to build and control railroads, canals, ports, and import/export houses.[18] Of course, the Hondurans began to make these concessions in the early 1900s, just as Teddy Roosevelt proclaimed the U.S. *right* to exercise an international police power in Central America— his "big stick" doctrine.

The banana industry grew rapidly in Honduras when the Americans took over. In 1892, bananas had accounted for only 11 percent of Honduran exports. By 1903, bananas were 42 percent of Honduran exports. And by 1913, bananas accounted for 66 percent of exports. In 1918, 75 percent of the banana-growing land in Honduras was owned by U.S. companies, which were ruthless in their efforts to get further favorable concessions from the Honduran government.[19]

American fruit companies invested in infrastructure, but their investments largely did not benefit the Honduran people. Northern Honduras, where bananas grow, was geographically and economically isolated from central and southern Honduras. Although the fruit companies built roads and railways linking the towns within the banana region, they built nothing in the rest of Honduras and did not link the banana region to the capital. It was easier to travel from Tela (in the banana region) to New Orleans, Louisiana (where several of the fruit companies were based), than from Tela to Tegucigalpa, the capital of the country. The banana companies paid little or no taxes to the Honduran government, so the people of Honduras benefitted little from their presence.[20]

---

18. Ibid., 22.
19. Ibid.
20. Ibid., 24.

The American banana companies were quite strategic in how they took advantage of Honduras's people, undeveloped economy, and weak political system. In 1911, Cuyamel Fruit Company, a New Orleans–based company founded by Samuel Zemurray, a Russian immigrant to the United States, suspected that then president Miguel Dávila's government was favoring United Fruit Company, a rival. (Some years later, Cuyamel Fruit Company was acquired by United Fruit.) Cuyamel responded to what it thought was favoritism with what turned into a presidential coup. Cuyamel recruited American "soldier of fortune" Lee Christian to lead the charge. Ultimately, the U.S. military stepped in to "restore stability" in Honduras, which meant that the United States replaced Dávila with a new president, Manuel Bonilla. Mr. Bonilla rewarded Cuyamel with concessions, including permission to build a new railroad line. In turn, Cuyamel loaned money to Mr. Bonilla to pay for the coup. And Lee Christian became the U.S. consul to Honduras.[21]

The attitude American businessmen had one hundred years ago toward the predecessors of the desperate Honduran migrants coming to the United States today can be seen clearly in a July 20, 1920, internal letter written by United Fruit executive H. V. Rolston to a colleague. Rolston wrote:

> Dr. Luis Melara
> San Pedro Sula
>
> Dear Luis,
> 1. In order that our great sacrifices and numerous investments have not been made in vain, we must take possession of as much state-owned and private land as possible, and acquire as much wealth as we have the capacity and power to absorb.
> 2. We must take every opportunity to enrich our company, and secure every possibility of exploiting new areas of operations. In short, we must acquire every piece of land that seems

---

21. Ibid., 25.

in accordance with our strategic interests and which guarantees our future progress and agricultural development, thus increasing our economic power.

3. We must draw up such irreversible contracts that nobody can compete with us, not even in the distant future; our aim is to ensure that whatever other company manages to establish itself and develop its operations, it will always fall under our control and adapt itself to our established principles.

4. We must secure concessions, privileges and exemptions from tariffs and custom duties; we must free ourselves of all public taxes and all those obligations and responsibilities which reduce our earnings and those of our associates. We must build for ourselves a privileged position with the aim of imposing our commercial philosophy and defending our economic interests.

5. It is indispensable to capture the imagination of these subjugated peoples, and attract them to the idea of our aggrandizement, and in a general way to those politicians and bosses that we must use. Observation and careful study have assured us that a people degraded by drink can be assimilated to the demands of necessity and destiny; it is in our interest to make it our concern that the privileged class, whom we will need for our exclusive benefit, bend itself to our will; in general, none of them has any conviction or character, far less patriotism; they seek only position and rank, and on being granted them, we will make them hungry for even more.

6. These men must not act on their own initiative, but rather according to determining factors and under our immediate control.

7. We must distance ourselves from those of our friends who have been in our service; we must consider them as degraded by their loyalty because sooner or later they will betray us; we must distance ourselves from those who feel offended and treat them with some deference, without being of any use to them. We do need their country, the natural resources of their coasts and ports, and little by little we must acquire them.

We are then at the point of departure; you know these men better than I. On your arrival, I will show you a list of the land we must obtain, if possible, immediately. . . .

Until we meet,
H.V. Rolston[22]

Ten years later, in 1930, Dr. Jose A. Lopez of the United Fruit Company's hospital at Puerta Castilla described Honduran workers in an internal report:

There is an air of dreaminess about them that verges on apathy, as they lounge in front of their camps. The insidious laziness is induced by impoverished blood, where the plasmodia of malaria have been playing havoc. . . . They lie in hammocks, smoking and looking at the sky; they sit on the railroad tracks and grunt as approaching trains disturb their repose.[23]

The Military

American involvement in Honduran affairs continued throughout the twentieth century, but the means evolved from bananas to the military. After World War II, Honduras remained, in terms of development, at the bottom of all Central American countries. Its economy continued to consist of the American-dominated banana plantations in the northern coastal area and subsistence farming throughout the rest of the country. The country lacked a central bank or even an income tax system, and its infrastructure remained poor. In the thirty years following World War II, the U.S.-nurtured Honduran military came to be the most powerful institution in the country.[24]

Unlike Guatemala and El Salvador, whose leaders had created professional armies loyal to them, the Honduran military arose inde-

---

22. Ibid., 23–24.

23. C. D. Kepner Jr., *Social Aspects of the Banana Industry* (New York: Columbia University Press, 1936).

24. Lapper and Painter, *Honduras*, 43–44.

pendent of any elite Honduran backers. Under a 1954 treaty, the United States promised to give Honduras military aid in exchange for virtually unlimited access to Honduran raw and semiprocessed materials. The United States set up military schools, granted scholarships, and supplied modern military equipment to nurture the Honduran military.[25]

Despite the fact that Hondurans were poorer than their neighbors and the country was ruled by a long line of corrupt leaders, Honduras did not experience rebellion and civil war, as did its neighbors, Guatemala, Nicaragua, and El Salvador. With at least the appearance of stability, the United States continued to gain influence in Honduras. When foreign companies were allowed to invest in Honduran financial institutions, the two largest banks in the country, Banco de Honduras and Banco Atlantida, came to be controlled by First City National Bank (1965) and Chase Manhattan (in 1967), respectively.[26]

In 1979, during the Cold War, U.S. president Jimmy Carter chose Honduras—the only Central American country not engulfed in civil war—to be the United States' "key ally" in the fight against "revolutionary communist movements" in the other countries in the region. Ronald Reagan, Carter's successor, is said to have viewed the Honduran/Nicaraguan border as the fourth border of the United States.[27] Mr. Reagan doubled down on Honduras. His administration turned the country into what was dubbed the "Pentagon Republic."

The Reagan administration pumped millions of dollars of military aid into Honduras. It simultaneously stationed thousands of American troops there to train fighters in the U.S. guerrilla action against the leftist Sandinistas, who had come to power in Nicaragua in 1979 after overthrowing the (U.S. Military Academy–trained) Nicaraguan dictator Anastasio Somoza. Honduras became the launching pad for the United States' determined effort to destabilize

---

25. Ibid., 45.
26. Ibid., 55.
27. Ibid., 74.

Nicaragua, financing and training the Contra forces who fought in Nicaragua. The Reagan administration also saw Honduras as a buffer against Communist forces in El Salvador.

Shared Goals

By the early 1980s, Honduras was effectively run by three men. The first was President Roberto Suazo Córdova. The second was General Gustavo Álvarez, the head of the Honduran military. Álvarez, who had as much influence as Suazo Córdova, had been trained in counterinsurgency by the U.S. Army at Fort Benning, Georgia, and at the U.S. Army School of the Americas in Panama. Álvarez expressed open admiration for the "dirty war" tactics of Chilean General Augusto Pinochet. The third man was U.S. ambassador John Negroponte, known for having facilitated increased American involvement in Vietnam during the Lyndon Johnson era and for having participated in the secret bombing of Cambodia by the United States.[28]

These three men openly shared the same goals: to destroy communism and to bring down the Sandinista government in Nicaragua. The Sandinistas, who had toppled the U.S.-trained dictator, Somoza, were named for Augusto César Sandino, who had led the Nicaraguan resistance against the U.S. occupation of Nicaragua in the 1930s. The Sandinistas were certainly not friendly toward U.S. interests. After Somoza's downfall, the United States backed a group known as the Contras, which fought to overthrow the Sandinistas, from the base of Honduras. American taxpayers' money funded this effort. Total military aid to Honduras in 1978 (during Carter's single term) had been $3.2 million, with total overall aid to the country at $16.2 million. In 1982, after Reagan took over, military spending shot up to $31 million (total aid was $109.4 million). By 1986, during Reagan's second term, military aid to Honduras was $88.2 million and total aid was $231.1 million.

---

28. Ibid., 82–83.

Post–Cold War Developments

Following the end of the Cold War, U.S. interest in fighting communism in Central America waned, and American dollars ceased to flow to Honduras at the prior levels. American-born gangs, deported from the United States, flooded into the country. Also entering the vacuum left by the Americans were the cartel drug-smuggling operations, facilitated by the Honduran military.[29]

Today, corruption in the Honduran government continues to be massive and uncontrolled. In 2015, the Honduran public engaged in a series of mass demonstrations demanding an end to corruption after it was revealed that former President Porfiro Lobo (2010–2014) had embezzled more than $300 million from the Honduran social security administration, and that some of the stolen funds were used to fund his successor, President Hernández's 2013 election campaign. Citizens demanded the creation of an international anticorruption organization (like the U.N.-backed CICIG in Guatemala). Not surprisingly, President Hernández would not allow an independent organization like CICIG in Honduras. Nevertheless, in 2016, a more limited anticorruption organization called Mission to Support the Fight against Corruption and Impunity in Honduras (MACCIH) was formed in conjunction with the Organization of American States. The U.S. Congressional Research Service reports that Honduras's Congress responded to MACCIH by repeatedly delaying and weakening MACCIH's reforms and hindering its mission. MACCIH was terminated in January 2020.[30]

Not surprisingly, Honduras lacks a system to protect neglected and abused children like Liliana. UNICEF reported that, thanks to funding from the government of Canada in 2017, the year Liliana

---

29. Julie Marie Bunck and Michael Ross Fowler, *Bribes, Bullets and Intimidation: Drug Trafficking and the Law in Central America* (University Park, PA: Penn State University Press, 2012), 258.

30. Hector Silva Avalos and Seth Robbins, "A Death Foretold: MACCIH Shuts Down in Honduras," In Sight Crime, January 22, 2020, https://www.insightcrime.org.

left her home, Honduras had finally made progress toward establishing a nationwide child protection system.[31] Liliana had no safety net to protect her in her own country.

Hondurans who flee their country today are escaping very real threats to their lives. And yet, enraged at the number of suffering Hondurans at the southern border, the Trump administration announced in March 2019 that it intended to end all foreign assistance to Honduras.[32] In July 2019, the administration announced its intention to send asylum seekers from Honduras to Guatemala as a "safe third country."[33] One month after Honduran President Hernández was named as a co-conspirator in a major federal drug trafficking case in New York, the administration announced, on September 25, 2019, that it had entered into a "safe third country" agreement with President Hernández. The administration's plan is to send asylum seekers from countries south of Honduras (such as Nicaragua and Venezuela) back to Honduras.[34] The various Trump administration strategies toward Hondurans will do nothing to end the exodus of suffering people from the country.

31. *UNICEF Annual Report 2017, Honduras*, https://www.unicef.org.

32. Meyer, "Honduras," 13.

33. Kirk Semple, "The U.S. and Guatemala Reached an Asylum Deal: Here's What It Means," *New York Times*, July 28, 2019, https://www.nytimes.com.

34. Nick Miroff, "U.S. Announces Asylum Deal with Honduras, Could Send Migrants to One of the World's Most Violent Nations," *Washington Post*, September 25, 2019, https://www.washingtonpost.com.

9

Federico and Camille Flores

In the summer of 2018, Federico and Camille Flores, a married couple, came in desperation from Guatemala to the U.S. border. Federico was forty-three years old and Camille was forty. Back in Guatemala, their son, Marco, had been brutally murdered as he sat chatting with one of his sisters. With Federico and Camille were their three surviving daughters: Sara, age sixteen; Daniela, age twelve; and Anita, age six.

They did not know it, but they had walked head on into the Trump administration's policy of "zero tolerance," under which children were being forcibly separated from their parents at the border. Under the policy, these children were declared to be "unaccompanied" and sent to juvenile detention centers so that their parents could be prosecuted criminally and then deported.

What would lead a family to leave everything they had and everyone they knew behind, travel thousands of miles, and beg to start over? In the case of the Flores family, it was loss, fear, despair, and a drive to save the lives of three young girls.

Family Neighborhood

The family had lived in a small village called Colonia El Mirador de San Cristobal, outside of Guatemala City. They owned a home, and Federico, a master builder, also supported the family with a second job driving a taxi. Camille took care of the family at home. As parents, homeowners, and community members, Federico and Camille were interested in keeping their neighborhood clean and safe. In

2016, they had formed a parents' committee with some neighbors to keep the neighborhood clean and their children safe. In time, they learned that business owners in nearby *colonias* (villages) had begun to receive threats from members of the Mara 18 gang. Mara 18 members had begun extorting business owners and assaulting people. The parents' committee feared that Mara 18 would soon try to move into their *colonia*.

The members spoke with the business owners about the gang problems they were facing. They learned that the police in the area were themselves already working with the Mara 18 members and could not be relied on for help. In January 2017, the parents' committee held a meeting, at which they decided to become a more active and visible "neighborhood watch," because they couldn't count on the police to protect them. Federico and his son, Marco, were among the first to commit to the neighborhood watch, which consisted of about twenty men and their sons. They patrolled the *colonia* every night, walking the neighborhood from 8:00 pm to 2:00 am. Another group of about ten men stood guard by the main entrance to the *colonia*, checking identification to prevent gang members from coming in.

The neighborhood watch was loosely structured—there was no one leader. But because they regularly patrolled the *colonia* in a group, it was easy to see and recognize who the neighborhood watch members were. They were the only large group of people who walked around at night. The men each carried something to defend themselves, like a bat, machete, or stick, but they did not have guns. They were family men and their sons, trying to keep the neighborhood safe for everyone.

One day, while Federico was driving his taxi, he was stopped by two men who had "18" tattoos on their arms and wore flat hats, loose pants and shirts, and chains around their necks—a look that is characteristic of Mara 18 members. The men told Federico that they knew he was part of the neighborhood watch and that he had information on the members. Federico denied being part of the watch, but they didn't believe him. They just stared at him and made hand gestures to indicate that they were keeping an eye on him. Federico and Marco continued to participate in the watch anyway.

Remembering Marco

On Friday, April 28, 2017, the lives of everyone in the Flores family changed forever. Camille's mother, Francisca, whom the children called "Pancha," was dying of cancer. She lived in a nearby *colonia*, and Camille and the children often spent time at her home caring for her in her last days. Camille's grown sisters and brothers were often there as well. On that afternoon, Camille had arrived at her mother's house around 2:30 pm. Twelve-year-old Daniela usually went to Pancha's house with her mother after school, but that day, she stayed home to ride her bicycle. Federico was driving his taxi.

The Flores family members always stayed in close touch by phone and by text. Around 4 pm, Camille called Federico to let him know that their son, Marco, had arrived at Grandma's house with Anita, and that they were all waiting for Sara to arrive from school as well. At around 4:45 pm, Sara called her dad to say that she was at her grandmother's house too. While Federico was on the call with Sara, he heard loud noises—what sounded like firecrackers—through the phone. He frantically asked Sara, "What happened, what happened?" He could only hear screaming on the line. Federico kept asking and saying, "Hello, hello," but all he could hear were screams. Federico hung up and tried to call Camille, but no one answered. Everything froze in time for Federico as a sense of dread washed over him. He was about forty-five minutes away but rushed to get to his mother-in-law's house. He got there in thirty minutes. During the drive, Federico's mind could not stop racing. He quietly cried.

For Marco, that Friday started out as any ordinary school day. At seventeen, he was a friendly and rather typical high-school student, distinguished by his green eyes and curly hair. Marco had a part-time job at McDonald's, but had quit when his parents decided he should focus on school. Marco played on a soccer team and enjoyed weight lifting. He was proud to be part of the neighborhood watch with his father and the other dads in the *colonia*.

That particular Friday, Marco had planned to go to his grandma's house after school to help his mom, Camille. He stopped at home first to pick up his youngest sister, Anita. Marco and Anita hopped on the bus together for the ten-minute ride to Grandma's house. When they arrived, Marco took his little sister inside to greet their mom and grandma. Then, Marco went back out front to sit on the porch. Soon, Sara arrived. She too went inside to say hello to everyone but then joined Marco on the front porch. Six-year-old Anita stayed in the living room with Camille and her grandma. Camille glanced out the living room window at Marco and Sara relaxing and laughing together. Marco smiled when he caught his mother's eye and gestured as if he was saying, "What?" Camille waved back that it was nothing and turned to walk toward her mother. She had gone only a few steps when the shooting began.

Sara, who was sixteen years old, adored her older brother, Marco. Always a strong student with an aptitude for math and computer programming, Sara attended the same high school as Marco. When she arrived at Grandma's house that Friday afternoon, she saw Marco sitting in front of the house. She knew that she would join him after she first went into the house to say hello to everyone. Sara was sitting with Marco, checking in with their dad on her phone when two men walked up to them from down the street. Sara realized they looked like gang members, but, before she even knew what was happening, the two lifted up their shirts a little to reveal their guns.

Sara was terrified and sat still with her phone at her ear, but Marco leaped up and tried to run. The two men shot him from only a few feet away. Sara sat frozen until Camille burst out of the house and ran straight to Marco. Camille threw herself over Marco. Her brother, Eddy, who had run out after her, tried to pull her away. But Camille had seen Marco open his eyes and knew he was still alive. She would not let go. Camille hugged and kissed Marco in her arms. She offered him to God. Marco stopped breathing. Sara, watching everything, could not think or feel. She was numb and in shock, and she remained seated. When the shooters ran down the street, Sara could only hear her father's voice repeatedly asking, "What happened?"

The scene was horrific when Federico arrived. People were still screaming, and Federico immediately saw Camille holding Marco in her lap. Marco was dead. Federico started crying again and ran to them. He desperately wanted Marco to wake up, to respond. No one said much to Federico. He felt hopeless and helpless. Sara, in anguish, explained to Federico what had happened. He felt rage. Federico asked Sara where the men had gone, and she pointed up the street. Federico went looking for them, walking around several blocks of houses, but he didn't find anyone.

All this time, Daniela was happily riding her bike in the neighborhood around the family's home. Suddenly, she noticed a neighbor crying. The woman approached Daniela and asked, "Didn't your mom call you?" She responded, "No, why?" The neighbor said, "Your brother is gone." The woman handed Daniela a phone to call her mother, but no one answered, so Daniela and the neighbor took the bus to Pancha's house. When they arrived, people were everywhere. Daniela couldn't see anything. They slowly moved closer, and finally, Federico pulled Daniela into his arms. She saw her brother lying on the ground and cried.

Eventually, the police came and casually asked Camille, Sara, and Federico some basic questions about Marco, such as his name and age. But they left soon after, and they never did anything else to investigate the case. The police didn't arrange to have Marco's body taken away. Marco's body lay in the street for more than two hours until the public ministry that deals with dead bodies arrived. They told Federico to go with them to the morgue to identify the body.

Federico was left waiting at the morgue the entire night for the formal identification of Marco's body. There was no autopsy. At approximately 5 am, Federico was finally allowed to identify Marco. That was the last time Federico saw his son. After the identification, Federico was told to pay a funeral home immediately to retrieve Marco's body. At around 11 am, the day after Marco was killed, the funeral home retrieved his body to prepare it for the wake services that took place that afternoon and evening.

While Federico was accompanying Marco's body, Camille and her daughters remained at Grandma's house with the other family members. They tried to get some sleep. The next day, Camille and the three girls were sitting in front of Grandma's house waiting for the funeral home to bring Marco's body for the wake. Suddenly, two men walking on the other side of the street snapped photos of them sitting there. Sara noticed the men when she saw the flash of a camera. Camille immediately herded the girls into the house. For the first time, through the fog of her grief, Sara felt fear; the initial shock had worn off. After that, Camille's brother, Eddy, noticed through the front window that a car with darkened windows was going up and down the street. Someone was keeping an eye on the house. During the wake, which was held at Grandma's house, Sara herself saw a car with dark, tinted windows going up and down the street again and again. When he heard this, Federico felt a new fear of the gang attacking the rest of his family.

Marco was buried the following day. Federico asked the police to protect the family at the burial. The police sent a single patrol car to the cemetery. After that, the Flores family returned to their own home. Camille went straight to Marco's room. She clung to the sheets on his bed. She didn't want to leave his belongings. Camille was afraid for her family and worried that at any moment they could all be killed, but she still did not want to leave Marco's room. Federico got her to drink something to calm her, but it did nothing.

Mara 18

Federico had always known that the police in Guatemala are corrupt and that they conspire with gangs. Those officers who are not corrupt are too scared to do anything when gangs are involved in a crime. Federico had no real hope that the police would do anything about Marco's murder. In fact, it is common knowledge that, when a gang crime occurs or someone is murdered, the police show up very late—after the gang members have all left—if they come at all. Ordinary people well know that, even when the police actually fill out paperwork for a case, like they did for Marco's murder, they don't actually investigate it.

On the morning after the family returned to their own home, Federico was getting some things out of the car when two men wearing motorcycle helmets that obscured their faces approached him carrying guns. The men showed Federico photos of his family taken outside the grandmother's house. They told Federico that, if he had any further contact with the police, they would first kill Sara, because she had seen Marco die, and then the rest of the family. The men spoke in an obscene and menacing manner. They knew each family member's name and, obviously, how to find them.

Federico realized that his family would never be safe in their home or *colonia*. Camille and their three daughters packed bags and left their home in Colonia El Mirador de San Cristobal without telling anybody where they were going. During the next couple of weeks, they moved from inn to inn, making sure they weren't followed. Camille's brother, Eddy, reported that even weeks after Marco's death, gang members were still driving motorcycles up and down the block looking for them. Federico traded in his taxi, worried that Mara 18 members or police would recognize his car.

While they moved from place to place, Federico always had Marco in the back of his mind. He was scared but felt he had to be strong for his family. His girls needed him to work so they would have enough money to stay on the move and to buy basic necessities. Federico called and texted his wife constantly throughout the day, making sure that she and the girls were safe in each place they stayed. Federico came and left late at night and made sure he was not watched.

A family friend, who was Daniela's and Anita's godfather, offered to let the family stay in two rooms in a house his brother owned in another town. Federico gratefully accepted. The two rooms weren't connected to each other but were separated by a hallway. Federico, Camille, and little Anita stayed in one room, while Sara and Daniela stayed in the other. There was a small refrigerator, a stove, and a dining table in the hallway between the rooms. Camille and the girls stayed there all the time, in hiding. Only Federico went out, and only to work. One day in May, people were setting off fireworks for Mother's Day. Camille found Anita huddled under a blanket, crying. Anita thought that the fireworks were gunshots and that the men who killed Marco were looking to kill the whole family.

On her birthday, Federico and Camille allowed Sara, a teenager who had been living in fear and isolation for months, to check her social media as a treat. Sara saw that two of her friends had posted that a man on a motorcycle had been asking about Sara at school. The man was interested in finding out where she had gone. Sara had a bad feeling when she saw the social media posts. After that, she wasn't allowed to access social media again, but she no longer even wanted to look at it or to go back to school to see her friends. Sara barely slept at night. Sometimes, she slept during the day, feeling slightly safer knowing her mom was awake, but she couldn't sleep at night when her parents were asleep. Sara kept re-living the moment of Marco's murder. Sometimes, she couldn't tell if she was having a nightmare or if she was awake.

About this time, the tombstone Federico had ordered for Marco's grave was ready. Camille's brother, Eddy, had gone to the cemetery a few weeks before to visit the gravesite. Eddy was there for about fifteen minutes when a man on a motorcycle came and stared at him. The man waited for about thirty minutes, just watching. Eddy believed the man was waiting to see if the rest of the family would arrive. After that, the family was desperately afraid to go to the cemetery, but they wanted to see Marco's headstone in place and say final goodbyes. They planned to sit by the grave and share stories about Marco. When they arrived at the cemetery, they were relieved to see another family sharing a picnic nearby at a different gravesite. That family's presence comforted them. After they had been there for half an hour or so, Federico went to buy some food. He thought the women would be safe because of the other family's close presence.

After Federico had gone, Camille noticed that a man, who had seemed to be with the other family, moved away from them. The man kept staring at Sara. He made a phone call. Shortly after that, another man cruised slowly into the cemetery on a motorcycle. The man parked close to the two families. He took off his helmet and unzipped a long cross-body bag slung over his shoulder. He loitered nearby as if waiting for a signal. Sara saw him reach into the bag and yelled that he had a gun. Camille grabbed Anita and they all ran.

Fernando found his family huddled behind the large pillars at the entrance of the cemetery. He saw the man on a motorcycle heading toward them. They all ran to the car and left the cemetery.

Federico and Camille knew then that the family had to leave Guatemala because Mara 18 was everywhere. But Camille still had obligations to her dying mother, and Federico needed to sell their house and save enough money for five people to travel. The house was slow to sell because the *colonia* was seen as dangerous. After Marco was killed, the neighborhood watch disbanded out of fear. Eventually the house sold. Federico went to the Public Ministry to get copies of the police report and documents about Marco's murder. He thought they might need them to obtain asylum in the United States.

The Journey to the United States

At the end of February 2018, the family started their journey. They traveled through Guatemala and Mexico together for two months, walking and taking buses when they could. When the family was on a bus in Mexico, between Monterey and the U.S. border at Nuevo Laredo, Mexican police stopped the bus. Officers boarded and took Federico and Daniela off the bus. They took them to the police station. Camille, Sara, and Anita were left on the bus and allowed to continue on the journey.

Mexican authorities questioned Federico and Daniela for two days. Eventually, after Federico showed them the documents he was carrying about Marco's murder, the Mexican authorities released them. But Federico and Daniela were stranded, separated from Camille and the other girls and unable to communicate with them. They continued to the United States–Mexico border alone.

Meanwhile, Camille, Sara, and Anita had continued on to the border crossing at Nuevo Laredo, Texas, where Camille asked for asylum in the second week of May 2018. She was given a "credible fear" interview, during which she explained what had happened to her family and why they were all afraid to return to Guatemala. Camille passed the credible fear test. After nineteen days in a family detention center with her two girls, all three were given a "notice to appear" in an unspecified immigration court on an unspecified date in the future. They were released into the United States and continued on their journey to Los Angeles, where a cousin lived.

The Pain of Separation

On May 16, 2018, just a few days after Camille and the girls had asked for asylum at Laredo, Texas, Federico and Daniela arrived in the same place. They encountered something completely different. Federico and Daniela walked up to the official crossing point and asked for asylum in the manner allowed under U.S. law. They were immediately detained in a cell at the border station with about twenty-five other people—adults and children. They stayed in this very cold cell for eight or nine hours. All the adults, including Federico, were told to fill out forms for themselves and their children.

Federico filled out Daniela's forms first. When he finished, and as he was about to start on his own forms, an immigration officer grabbed one of Daniela's arms and pulled her away. The officer brusquely announced that he was taking Daniela to an area with other youth. Daniela immediately started crying. Shaking, she said she did not want to be taken from her father. She grabbed onto Federico and would not let go. Federico asked where the officer wanted to take Daniela. He told the officer that, since Daniela was only twelve years old, she had to stay with him. The man wasn't interested. He responded firmly that he was taking Daniela, and that they might tell Federico something later. As Daniela was led away, she looked at Federico sadly with tears streaming down her face.

In that moment, Federico felt truly hopeless. He was alone in a strange and hostile place, and there was nothing he could do to protect his daughter. He was scared and angry, but he felt completely powerless. The officer had behaved aggressively. He made it plain that the officers were the only ones with power, and they could not be stopped. Federico was also embarrassed to be in a situation where he was helpless to do what he believed a father should do for his daughter. Although he had no choice, he felt he had let the officer take his child away. When Federico had decided with Camille to bring their children to the U.S. border to ask for help, Federico had never dreamed that the United States would take his child away from him. He feared he would never see Daniela again.

The Experience of Detention Centers

But Federico's difficulties were just beginning. He was put in a cell with other distraught adults, whose children had also been taken from them. None of them knew where their children were. Federico begged the officers who walked by the cell every few hours to tell him what they had done with Daniela, but the officers didn't even bother to respond. They ignored Federico and the other people shouting questions about their children. At about 3:00 am on the morning after Daniela was taken from Federico, all the children in detention were lined up outside. The captive adults saw their children through a window of their cell. The parents pounded on the cell door to ask what was happening, but again, none of the officials responded. The children were marched out of sight. Hours later, around 9 am, an officer brought some food. The parents begged for answers about their children, but the officer said he didn't know anything. After that, they waited another sixteen hours before they were moved to formal detention centers where they were separated by gender.

The conditions Federico and the other adults experienced in this cell at the border station were extremely difficult. The cell was chilled and cramped. Federico was given only a Mylar sheet to hold around himself for warmth. There was no place to lie down. In the twenty-four hours Federico was there, he was given food only twice, and he was given only a small bottle of water at each meal. Federico slept very little and what time he did sleep was on the cold concrete floor. Using the restroom was difficult because the people had to wait for an officer to walk by the cell and then get the officer's attention. One woman had to use the restroom very badly. She knocked on the door three different times and yelled to the officers that she needed to go. They ignored her. She ended up soiling her clothes and sat in shame, while the others tried to ignore the situation.

After a day at the border station, Federico was moved to Rio Grande Detention Center, a privately owned, for-profit prison in Laredo, Texas. The facility is run by the GEO Group, one of the country's largest private, for-profit prison operators. But no one told Federico where they were taking him, or why. He asked if Daniela would be waiting for him. The officers said no, but in the new place, men and women would be separated.

To make the transfer to the Rio Grande Detention Center, officers handcuffed Federico behind his back and placed him in leg chains. That meant cuffs on his hands and feet, with two short chains connecting both hands together with his feet. The chains made the law-abiding Federico, who had never been in trouble in his life, feel deeply ashamed. He could not fathom why he was being treated this way. The officials manhandled Federico onto a transport vehicle. The cuffs and chains left marks that lasted for days.

When Federico and the other detainees arrived at Rio Grande Detention Center, they were taken into cells, one by one. Officers asked them questions and took down information. But the officers told Federico they did not know anything about Daniela. No one told him anything about how he could get out of prison. Federico saw posters on the walls in English and Spanish that described how to ask questions. Federico filled out a form asking for information about Daniela, and another requesting information about Camille and his other two daughters. He included all the information he had. After five days, Federico received a response stating that Daniela was in a detention center for minors in San Antonio, Texas. He was not allowed to contact her, and he was not allowed to receive phone calls. Federico never received any response to his request for information about Camille.

Federico was held in the Rio Grande Detention Center for two-and-a-half weeks, not knowing why he was there. After that, without explanation, he was moved again; this time to Stewart Detention Center. Stewart is located in Lumpkin, Georgia, more than a thousand miles from Rio Grande. It is one of the most notorious for-profit prisons in the country, run by a competitor of GEO called CoreCivic. Prisoners at Stewart can have toothpaste, if they can buy it, for eleven dollars a tube.[1] During the long drive to Georgia, Federico was again cuffed, placed in leg chains, and generally treated like a criminal. He had done nothing other than approach a U.S. official border crossing and ask for asylum.

At the Stewart Detention Center, Federico became ill. He couldn't eat much and was too sick to go out into the yard. He didn't know anyone and had no one he could trust to talk to. Federico tried to sleep at night, but thoughts of Marco, Camille, Sara, and Anita, and finally Daniela, being stripped away from him one by one, kept him awake. Some of the other prisoners played cards and talked at night, and that also kept Federico awake. He slept in brief spurts during the day.

Federico had severe and frequent headaches, mostly behind his left eye. It was a very strong pain that left him debilitated. He had a high fever. The rooms at Stewart were very cold, and Federico had chills and body aches. His hair was falling out, and he was covered with hives. His stomach ached, and he had symptoms of a urinary tract infection. Federico lost eight pounds during the first two weeks he was incarcerated at Stewart.

Not surprisingly, Federico was increasingly unwell psychologically, too. He was desperate to know what had happened to his family. He was anxious and irritable all the time, constantly having the same desperate thoughts. His anguish at not knowing about his family left him feeling helpless and depressed because he could not think of anything he could do for them or himself.

After two weeks at Stewart, Federico was inexplicably transferred—in full chains again—to a place called Folkston Immigration Processing Center, another GEO for-profit prison in Georgia, about two hundred miles from Stewart. After another ten disorienting days at Folkston, Federico was transferred in chains back to Stewart, where he was imprisoned for another month and a half.

---

1. Anhelica Robles, "Behind the Gates of Stewart Detention Center," SPCL Southern Poverty Law Center, February 28, 2019, https://www.splcenter.org.

At both of the Georgia detention centers, Federico was too scared to ask to see a doctor or a nurse. Prisoners knew that if you asked for a doctor, you would often end up in isolation in a locked room. Once a man was in isolation, he would be there twenty-four hours a day. Federico heard that sometimes men were kept in isolation for more than a month. Rumors like these served to keep costs down by dissuading prisoners from utilizing medical services. No prison staff person ever asked about Federico's health or his obviously deteriorating condition.

Christian services were held at Stewart once a week. Federico attended, and he read the Bible to keep his mind busy. He focused only on two questions: When would he see his family and when could he get out of prison? He couldn't stop the nightmare thought that he would never see his family again. Federico heard that prisoners in Folkston and Stewart had hung themselves. He understood what led them to do this, and he prayed to avoid thoughts of suicide.

The Interview Process

At Folkston, Federico was interviewed over the telephone about his request for asylum. Unlike the in-person "credible fear" interview Camille had been given, Federico's telephone interview was done by a woman who did not speak Spanish. Every question required a translator, who was also on the telephone but in a third location. The interview felt very impersonal to Federico. The interviewer asked primarily "yes" or "no" questions, but if Federico did not understand something, the interviewer moved on—she would not repeat the question. Federico wanted to explain that he left everything behind in Guatemala because he and his family were terribly persecuted there because of the neighborhood watch, that his son had been murdered, and that he feared that he and his family would be killed if they returned. But he never got a chance to tell his story. It was difficult for Federico to communicate because he was so ill and stressed. Federico relived the horrifying experiences of Marco's murder and his separation from his family whenever he tried to speak of them.

Eight days after the interview, an ICE agent informed Federico, over the phone, that his fear was not credible. He was told that ICE had decided he did not qualify for asylum. The agent on the phone said that a different ICE agent would come to Federico's cell with more information. An ICE agent did, in fact, visit Federico in his cell and told him that it would be a waste of time to ask for an immigration judge to review the credible fear decision because American immigration judges always defer to ICE decisions. The ICE agent said that Federico's type of case was "personal" to ICE, and that the United States was not interested in giving asylum to people like Federico. The ICE agent gave Federico a paper—in English and without a translation—to sign that waived Federico's right to have his case reviewed by an immigration judge. The agent told Federico that, unless he signed the paper, there was no telling how long he would stay in prison.

When Federico heard that he had failed the credible fear interview, he was stunned. He couldn't understand how that could be so. He had believed that the American system was not corrupt, and he was terrified of returning to Guatemala. But the ICE agent was adamant that people like Federico could never get asylum in this country. Federico was deported to Guatemala on August 22, 2018. The experience of being separated from his family is the worst thing Federico can imagine anyone going through, apart from the searing experience of having a child murdered.

Camille and the Girls

What happened to Camille and the three girls? When Daniela was separated from Federico at the border station, she was taken to another room crowded with children. Some were crying, and others stood in silence. In the middle of the night, they were told to line up outside. Daniela felt despair, but she followed the group. She believed she would never see her father again, and she had no hope that she would ever be able to find her mother and sisters. Daniela was taken to an ORR shelter for unaccompanied minors—like Gilberto, Liliana, Gabriela, and Javi, who had made the journey to the United States without their parents. She was held there for more than a month, not knowing anything about her family members, even whether they were still alive.

Meanwhile, Camille, Sara, and Anita had found their way to Los Angeles and had moved into the one-bedroom apartment that Camille's niece shared with her husband and their small son. Camille, who by this time had lost her son and her mother, and had been separated from her husband and one of her daughters, was suffering from severe depression and shock. With the help of the agency KIND, which, in the summer of 2018, had expanded its mission to help separated families, Camille finally found out where Daniela was being held. Daniela was released from the ORR detention facility into her mother's custody. She joined her mother and sisters in Los Angeles. Camille and all three girls are in removal proceedings in immigration court in Los Angeles.

KIND found a team of pro bono lawyers for the family. The lawyers found a wonderful translator/mentor, Bertha Cardenti, who—like Martha DeLira—volunteers through the Archdiocese of Los Angeles. Slowly, the team learned the family's story and prepared applications for asylum for the four in the United States. They have all "pled to the charges" against them in immigration court and have filed extensive applications for asylum that detail their story and substantiate their claim with evidence. They are awaiting trial on their asylum claim, which will take place in 2020.

But Camille and the three girls were not thriving. All of them were suffering terribly from the devastating traumas they suffered in Guatemala, during their journey, and at the border. Camille, who had been a homemaker in Guatemala, had no money and was not allowed to work until her asylum case had been pending for six months. Camille finally learned that Federico was in jail in Georgia and that he would be deported. She despaired that, without Federico, the family could not survive.

Camille and her three daughters continued to struggle, but they were surrounded with love and support by many generous people—Catholics, Jews, Protestants, and "nones" in the city of Los Angeles.

The Archdiocese of Los Angeles helped the family find a place to live, and a private donor is subsidizing their rent while they go through the immigration court process. The Los Angeles Mayor's Office of Immigrant Affairs helped Camille navigate the school system. Camille and all three girls are receiving therapy at St. John's Well Child and Family Center. The family has been showered with furniture, clothing, and household supplies—so much so that they held a yard sale to dispose of some of the extra items. The little family has been befriended by other local families, including the family of Bertha Cardenti, who have shared holidays and other meals with them.

The girls are finding their places in their new schools. The people of Los Angeles, through their faith and good will, have welcomed this suffering stranger family and are holding them until they can be fully self-supporting members of the community. The little family has stabilized. But they would not be complete until Federico could join them to ask for asylum.

Federico remained in hiding, moving around from place to place in Guatemala. He saw his wife and daughter only on WhatsApp and yearned to be with them. Federico knew that his family was safe in the United States and that it would be dangerous for them to return to Guatemala, but he desperately wanted to be with them, to support them, and to watch his daughters grow up. The U.S. government continued to do everything in its power to keep Federico out.

Legal Injunction

On June 26, 2018, at the request of the ACLU, San Diego, California–based federal judge Dana Sabraw granted a nationwide injunction against the Trump administration's family separation policy, which affected Federico and his daughter, sending Daniela to a children's detention center and imprisoning and deporting him.[2] On the day Judge Sabraw ordered the injunction, Federico was

---

2. Judge Sabraw is a Republican, appointed to the federal bench by President George W. Bush in 2003.

still languishing in the Folkston Processing Center in Georgia. Five days before this order, Daniela had been released from detention and allowed to join Camille and her sisters in Los Angeles. Under the order, the government was enjoined from deporting Federico or parents like him. ICE deported Federico anyway.

Judge Sabraw's order did more than just stop the administration from separating children from their parents at the border. It required the government to find the many children who had been taken from parents *and reunite them.* In the wake of this order, the public was aghast to learn that the government had not even bothered to keep accurate track of the children and parents from whom they had been taken, which made reunification of parents and their children extremely difficult for the government.[3] The government's lawyers actually argued that because they hadn't kept track, it would be too difficult even to attempt reunification of the children with their parents, and they should not have to try.

In a follow-up order on August 3, 2018, Judge Sabraw ruled that it was indeed the government's obligation to find and reunite the separated children with their parents.[4] On the day of Judge Sabraw's second order, Federico was still languishing in the Stewart Detention Center in Georgia. But the government did not try to reunite him with Daniela. Instead, two months after Judge Sabraw's initial order and less than three weeks after his second order, the government deported Federico to Guatemala.

Three months later, Judge Sabraw entered a third order, approving an agreement between the government and the ACLU that was intended to give deported parents like Federico a second chance to apply for asylum in the United States with their families. By this time, the government had publicly admitted to having separated

3. See, e.g., Franco Ordonez and Anita Kumar, "Exclusive: U.S. Officials Likely Lost Track of Nearly 6,000 Unaccompanied Migrant Kids," McClatchy DC Bureau, June 19, 2018, https://www.mcclatchydc.com.

4. Lauren Pearle, "Judge Rejects Government Call for ACLU to Bear Reunification Responsibility," ABC News, August 3, 2018, https://abcnews.go.com.

more than 2,600 children from their parents.[5] That number turned out to be a significant undercount.[6]

Federico was overjoyed to learn that there was even a possibility that he might get a chance to be reunited with his family and seek asylum. The team of lawyers that already represented his family worked with Federico over the phone to prepare an application, telling the story of what the government had done to him. Federico waited anxiously in Guatemala. The government's first response was that, notwithstanding Federico's experience in U.S. custody, they did not even consider him to be a "separated parent." The government contended that since they had released Daniela to her mother a few days *before* Judge Sabraw's order about reuniting parents and children on June 26, 2018, Federico and Daniela were not a "separated family." The government said Federico could not even ask to be considered for reunification.

This nonsensical position led the ACLU and Federico's team to go back to Judge Sabraw, asking him to direct the government to identify and reunite all separated families, not just those who were still in U.S. custody on June 26, 2018. Judge Sabraw entered precisely this order in March 2019.[7] The government was ordered to treat Federico and Daniela as a separated family and to consider Federico's application to return to the United States to seek asylum. The government has been represented in this case before Judge Sabraw by, among others, a government attorney called Sarah

---

5. Joshua Barajas, "Judge Approves Settlement Giving Some Migrant Parents Second Chance at Asylum," PBS News Hour, November 16, 2018, https://www.pbs.org/newshour.

6. In a comprehensive report by the U.S. Department of Health and Human Services' Office of the Inspector General, titled "Many Children Separated from Parents, Guardians Before *Ms. L. v. ICE* Court Order and Some Separations Continue," January 17, 2019, the government reported that separations had begun long before previously admitted by the Trump administration and the previously official number of 2,737 was vastly underreported, https://www.oig.hhs.gov.

7. Julie Small, "Judge: Immigration Must Account for Thousands More Migrant Kids Split Up from Parents," NPR, March 19, 2019, https://www.npr.org.

Fabian, who became momentarily famous in June 2019 for arguing to judges of the Ninth Circuit Court of Appeals that detained children do not need soap, toothpaste, or to sleep in order to be in "safe and sanitary conditions."[8]

After Judge Sabraw directed the government to consider Federico—and other deported parents like him—for return and reunification, Ms. Fabian advised the ACLU that after "consideration," neither Federico *nor a single other deported parent* who had applied to be reconsidered would be allowed to return. Ms. Fabian advised that ICE concluded that neither Federico nor any other applicant had experienced anything "rare or unusual" and that none of them would be allowed to return to the United States to be reunited with their children and to apply for asylum.

This decision meant that the government saw the treatment Federico experienced in the detention centers in Georgia, where an ICE officer misrepresented to him that "immigration judges defer to the ICE," that Federico's kind of case was "personal" to ICE, and that the United States wasn't interested in giving asylum to "people like Federico" were run of the mill, business as usual. All of those things were actually against the law.

Ms. Fabian eventually told the ACLU that deported parents in Federico's situation could submit an application for something called "humanitarian parole," a complicated process that applies to foreign people who wish to enter the United States for a limited time for a humanitarian purpose, such as accompanying a relative through a surgery. That process is not applicable to people who wish to remain in the country to seek asylum. The parole process also requires applicants to provide proof that they will be supported financially during their visit to the country, something the law does not require of asylum applicants.

Even though the humanitarian parole process Ms. Fabian offered seemed inapplicable, Federico's lawyers prepared the burdensome

---

8. Manny Fernandez, "Lawyer Draws Outrage for Defending Lack of Toothbrushes in Border Detention," *New York Times*, June 25, 2019, https://www.nytimes.com.

application anyway—because the government had offered it. The Archdiocese of Los Angeles and Temple Israel of Hollywood provided the required letters of support for Federico. But it was for nothing. The government summarily rejected Federico's parole application and every other parole application submitted, without explanation.

On July 12, 2019, Judge Sabraw considered another motion by the ACLU to require the government to allow Federico and twenty-one other deported parents like him to return to the United States to be reunited with his family and to apply for asylum with them, based on the various violations of U.S. law they had experienced. On September 4, 2019, Judge Sabraw granted the motion as to Federico and ten other separated and deported parents. Judge Sabraw ruled explicitly that the government violated the law when it deported Federico in the summer of 2018, after Judge Sabraw had expressly ordered the government to cease the deportations of parents who had been separated from their children. Four months later, on January 22, 2020, Federico returned to the United States to pursue asylum. He joyfully reunited with Camille and her three daughters at Los Angeles International Airport. The family's claim for asylum is pending in immigration court in Los Angeles.

THE CATHOLIC WAY

The great truth which we learn from nature herself is also the grand Christian dogma on which religion rests as on its foundation—that, when we have given up this present life, then shall we really begin to live. God has not created us for the perishable and transitory things of earth, but for things heavenly and everlasting; He has given us this world as a place of exile, and not as our abiding place. As for riches and the other things which men call good and desirable, whether we have them in abundance, or are lacking in them—so far as eternal happiness is concerned— it makes no difference; the only important thing is to use them aright.

—Pope Leo XIII, *Rerum Novarum*,
May 1, 1891

THE CATHOLIC WAY

10

Pope Pius XII

Exsul Familia Nazarethana

In 1952, Pope Pius XII wrote the Catholic Church's definitive teaching document on immigration called *Exsul Familia Nazarethana*.[1] In the half-century that preceded *Exsul Familia*, two world wars had created millions of migrants and refugees in the world. In the wake of this devastation, the colonial relationships that had existed between various European countries and the rest of the world began to unravel. Borders, governments, and even the names of many countries changed. New countries came into being. Pius XII's *Exsul Familia* is an "apostolic constitution," the highest level of papal decree that was written to the universal church in a time of mass migration. It proudly sets forth the history of the church's centuries of "motherly solicitude" for migrants, calling the Holy Family of Nazareth fleeing into Egypt "the archetype of every refugee family."

In *Exsul Familia*, Pius XII expanded the church's teaching on *which* migrants Catholics must welcome and assist. Catholics must welcome not only people whose lives are in danger but also people who left their home countries "by want," to find work—because they could not sustain themselves or their families in their home countries. In other words, Catholics may not demonize migrants who cannot support themselves in their own countries and thus seek opportunities elsewhere by calling them "economic migrants."

---

1. Pius XII, *Exsul Familia Nazarethana*, August 1, 1952, http://www.papalencyclicals.net.

Exsul Familia does not permit Catholics to ignore their obligations by contending that "migrants' own countries should take responsibility for them." It does not allow Catholics to ignore suffering migrants by arguing that providing aid might create incentives for more suffering migrants to come. The document states that *Catholics help each migrating human being they encounter.* Always.

In *Exsul Familia*, Pius XII lamented that, just as he became pope (in 1939), "there daily appeared more bold and violent symptoms of unrestrained desire for extending national boundaries, for an idolized supremacy of rage . . . and for reliance on might rather than on right," which led to "the shameless deportation of entire nations and the forced migration of peoples."[2]

Pius XII mourned that this unrestrained nationalism had led to World War II's devastation, creating millions of migrants and refugees. He lauded the church's work on behalf of migrants and refugees "in every country, indeed in almost every diocese" in the world.

Calling it the "custom of the Catholic Church to provide assistance for the wretched and the abandoned," Pius XII wrote that he had "tried earnestly to produce in the minds of all people a sympathetic approach toward exiles and refugees who are our needier brothers."[3] He continued, "We have repeatedly addressed the Rulers of States, the heads of agencies and all upright and cooperative men, urging upon them the need to consider and resolve the very serious problems of refugees and migrants." He urged leaders to "harmonize the requirements of justice with needs of charity."[4] Sixty years later, the world is not listening, as Pope Francis urges the same things.

Natural Law

Pius XII instructed Catholics that the right to migrate is found in natural law. The periodic need of all humans to migrate is part of our God-given human nature. In contrast, "borders" and "nations" are entirely human constructs that, as World War II demonstrated,

---

2. Ibid., Title 1.
3. Ibid.
4. Ibid.

change over time, because humans are fallible. Quoting from his own June 1, 1951, speech on the fiftieth anniversary of Pope Leo XII's encyclical *Rerum Novarum*,[5] Pope Pius's apostolic constitution *Exsul Familia* stated that, given the nature of our planet, with regions both habitable and not habitable, "it is inevitable, that some families migrating from one spot to another should go elsewhere in search of a new homeland."[6]

Remaining consistent with *Rerum Novarum*, Pius XII further proclaimed that the right of a family to be together is fundamental to the natural law. He wrote that there are people "who have been forced, by such things as war, unemployment and hunger, to leave their homes and live in foreign lands," and "the natural law itself, no less than devotion to humanity, urges that ways of migration be opened to these people."[7]

Pius XII, and every pope who has followed him in the twentieth and twenty-first centuries, acknowledged that sovereign countries have borders. He acknowledged that political leaders are obligated to protect the people within their borders as part of seeking the common good. But Pius XII understood, as did Thomas Aquinas before him, that common good does not mean we circle the wagons and protect only the people who already happen to be in a particular place at a particular moment in history. It means that our leaders and our laws must ensure that every human person has a way to seek God and God's will.

The Common Good

Common good has nothing to do with an "America first" attitude. It is not concerned with protecting a standard of living or a way of life—at the expense of decent people from across a border. Pius XII and each of his successors have made abundantly clear the priority between the competing needs of nations to enforce their borders,

---

5. Leo XIII, *Rerum Novarum* (On Capital and Labor), May 15, 1891, http://w2.vatican.va.

6. Pius XII, *Exsul Familia*, Title 1.

7. Ibid.

on the one hand, and our Christian obligation to care for suffering migrants, on the other:

> The sovereignty of the State, although it must be respected, cannot be exaggerated to the point that access to this land is, for inadequate or unjustified reasons, denied to needy and decent people from other lands, provided of course, that the public wealth, considered very carefully, does not forbid this.[8]

Catholics may never legitimately conclude that decent suffering people—like Liliana or the Flores family—can be ignored or turned away, because "the Church says that the State is entitled to protect its borders as it sees fit." That argument is simply not the Catholic way.

Nor may Catholics support laws or leaders who engage in what Pius called "exaggerated nationalism," which "arbitrarily restrict[s] the natural rights of people to migrate."[9] The refusal to accept a share of the refugees in the world is contrary to natural law and Catholic teaching. Yet, the Trump administration has drastically slashed refugee admissions to the country, claiming that taking refugees under a global compact for migration is inconsistent with U.S. sovereignty, the position first articulated by then U.S. ambassador to the United Nations Nikki Haley in 2017, when withdrawing the United States from the global compact for migration.[10]

The United States allowed 110,000 refugees to be admitted to the country in 2016. Mr. Trump slashed that number to a maximum of 30,000 shortly after he took office. In November 2019, the Trump administration announced that the number would be further slashed to 18,000. In the summer of 2019, it was reported that the Trump administration intended to "zero out" the number of refugees that the United States would accept entirely. Not surprisingly, this announcement prompted immediate outrage from the U.S. Conference of Catholic Bishops. Bishop Joe S. Vasquez

---

8. Ibid.

9. Ibid.

10. Rick Gladstone, "U.S. Quits Migration Pact, Saying It Infringes on Sovereignty," *New York Times*, December 3, 2017, https://www.nytimes.com.

of Austin, Texas, the chair of the USCCB's Conference on Migration immediately called out this strategy: "Eliminating the refugee resettlement program leaves refugees in harm's way and keeps their families separated across continents."[11]

In *Exsul Familia*, Pius XII severely condemned totalitarian and imperialistic states that restrict natural law rights of people—like the policies of the Trump administration. Pius XII stated that "those in need, whose own lands lack the necessities of life," should be allowed "to emigrate to other countries."[12]

The Message for Today

What does *Exsul Familia*—the Catholic Church's magnum opus on migration—say to American Catholics today? It says that suffering people who are persecuted for any reason (not just the five precise reasons allowed under current asylum law) and impoverished people who cannot support themselves in their own lands have a natural law right to migrate. Catholics in lands of plenty like the United States must recognize natural law as God's way and welcome such people as if they were the Holy Family escaping to Nazareth.

No Catholic, and indeed no Christian, may legitimately argue that "Americans" or "Poles" or "Germans" or any other country's current residents "come first" over other children of God. No Catholic may use a "slippery slope" form of argument that we have to turn desperate people back to where they came from, or else too many more of these people will follow them and our standard of living might be impacted. These arguments are contrary to Scripture, contrary to natural law, and against the teaching of our faith.

Since Pope Leo XIII's encyclical *Rerum Novarum*, at the end of the nineteenth century, the church has taught consistently that although the right to private property is a principle of the natural law, our lives are *not* ultimately about amassing riches or protect-

---

11. Julie Asher, "Update: Agencies 'Appalled' by Reports U.S. Could End Refugee Admissions," Catholic News Service, July 19, 2019, https://www.catholicnews.com.

12. Ibid.

ing standards of living. Leo XIII wrote that humans are not created for "the perishable and transitory things of earth," but for life with God. Accordingly, the church teaches that the whole point of private property is that it provides us with an opportunity "to use [it] aright" (no. 21). The church, therefore, has long taught that once a person has enough to take care of himself and his household, it becomes a duty and is part of perfecting one's nature to give to the indigent what is left over (no. 22).

11

Pope Saint John Paul II

In the spring and summer of 2018, the American public was simultaneously captivated and appalled by the news that, at the direction of then attorney general Jeff Sessions, the United States had implemented the new "zero tolerance" policy of taking children (like Daniela) from the arms of their parents, like Federico, with whom they approached the border, charging the parents with criminal violation of U.S. law (for entering the country), deporting the parents, and leaving the children in ORR juvenile detention facilities.

The Trump Administration's Family Separation Policy

Ghastly media images of young children crying or sitting silently in cages, separated from their poor, distraught parents, led even those who supported the administration's anti-immigrant stance to cry foul. San Diego federal judge Dana Sabraw issued an order on June 26, 2018, halting the family separation practice in a case known as *Ms. L. v. ICE.*[1] Judge Sabraw actually ordered the Trump administration to find all the children who had been separated from a parent at the border and reunite them. In response to Judge Sabraw's order, the government initially certified to the court in July 2018 that it had taken 2,654 children from their parents. The government revised that number periodically, ultimately certifying that 2,737 children had been separated. That number also turned out to be untrue.

---

1. Judge Sabraw's order allowed the government to continue the longstanding *but limited* practice of separating children from adults when there was a legitimate reason to suspect the adults of trafficking or other serious criminal conduct.

In January 2019, the inspector general of the U.S. Department of Health and Human Services (HHS), which is responsible for ORR juvenile detention facilities, released a damning report, revealing that the Trump administration had been separating children from their parents at the border since mid-2017, months before Mr. Sessions formally announced the practice in April 2018.[2] But the government had not admitted it had been taking children from their parents since 2017, and it had not included the children taken before the formal announcement of the policy in 2018 in reports it provided to Judge Sabraw on how many children had been separated.

In response to another motion by the ACLU, and over strenuous objection by government attorneys, Judge Sabraw ordered the government to find all of the children who had been separated from their parents. At the hearing in San Diego on March 9, 2019, Judge Sabraw stated:

> When there is an allegation of wrongdoing on this scale, one of the most fundamental obligations of the law is to bring to light what that wrong was and what is the scope of the wrong.[3]

The Trump administration's family separation strategy and what motivated it will stand as one of the darkest moments in modern U.S. history. The long-term consequences to the children who were forcibly taken from their parents by adults in police uniforms will only be fully known over their lifetimes. Child development experts opine that the sudden and forcible separation of a child from her parent, such as Mr. Sessions carried out, can cause developmental, psychological, and physical damage to babies, school-age children, and teens that will plague the children for the rest of their lives.[4]

2. U.S. Department of Health and Human Services Office of Inspector General, "Many Children Separated," https://www.oig.hhs.gov.

3. Julie Small, "Judge: Immigration Must Account for Thousands More Migrant Kids Split Up from Parents," NPR, March 9, 2019, https://www.npr.org.

4. Katie Scott, "'A Blanket of Fear': How Deportations Affect Children," Catholic Sentinel, July 26, 2019, https://www.catholicsentinel.org.

Nevertheless, some people, including Catholics, contend that, at the end of the day, the parents were to blame for bringing their children to the border in the first place. Such people claim that since the parents are to blame, the government was right to take the children from them. In this way, Americans avoid having to face what Scripture and Catholic teaching say about welcoming the suffering stranger.

The Trump administration's many policies since 2017 are explicitly intended to be deterrents to Central Americans coming to the United States. The administration simply does not want poor Central Americans to come to this country, regardless of the threats to life they are facing. Both Mr. Sessions and former secretary of the Department of Homeland Security (DHS) and White House chief of staff General John F. Kelly readily admitted that the zero tolerance family separation strategy was intended to deter desperate families from coming to the United States.

General Kelly, a Catholic, well knew that Central Americans who come to the United States are fleeing terrible violence and atrocities at home. Nevertheless, he stated that with the family separation strategy, "a big name of the game is deterrence," and "it could be a tough deterrent—would be a tough deterrent."[5] But as Catholics, we may not avoid the sad gaze of Jesus by telling ourselves, "These suffering people should go somewhere else," or "This is the law, it must be right," or "These immigrants are law breakers so they should be punished."

The Legal Position on Family Separation

First, it is legal for anyone to ask for asylum at the border of the United States. Moreover, Judge Sabraw's orders and the report of the HHS inspector general readily demonstrated that it was the Trump administration's family separation policy that was against

---

5. Philip Bump, "Here Are the Administration Officials Who Have Said That Family Separation Is Meant as a Deterrent," *Washington Post*, June 19, 2018, https://www.washingtonpost.com.

the law, not the requests for asylum. The court ordered that the administration's separations must cease and the children must be reunited with their parents, because the separations were contrary to U.S. law.

Second, for people who are fleeing for their very lives, are looking for a way to keep themselves and their children from being killed, or are trying to find a way to earn enough money to keep their children from starving, even if U.S. law had allowed the separations, which it didn't, a law that would punish people for asking for help is—in the words of Thomas Aquinas—"no law at all." Catholics today, like those who defied slavery or aided their Jewish neighbors in World War II Europe, must help these people preserve their lives and safeguard their children.

Centesimus Annus

In 1991, two years before his encyclical *Veritatis Splendor*, Pope John Paul II released the encyclical *Centesimus Annus*, on issues of social and economic justice. Throughout *Centesimus Annus*, John Paul II called on the world's leaders to be the agents of justice for the poor and to defend human rights. He affirmed the dogma of the faith that the transcendent human dignity of every human person must be protected in every situation[6] and confirmed that every person has a "grave obligation" to ensure the preservation of life, and that *every individual* has a natural right to migrate and work in order to procure what is required to live (cf. no. 8).

In *Centesimus Annus*, John Paul II taught that the defenseless and the poor, like Gilberto, Gabriela, Javi, Liliana, and the Flores family, have a claim to special consideration from us as Catholic Christians. John Paul II had no interest whatsoever in defending nationalism, in separating people by borders, or in mandating that governments should take care of their own. John Paul II instead taught that our duty to protect the transcendent human dignity of every person

---

6. John Paul II, *Centesimus Annus* (On the Hundredth Anniversary of *Rerum Novarum*), May 1, 1991, no. 5, http://w2.vatican.va.

extends progressively *to all mankind*, since no one can consider himself extraneous or indifferent to the lot of another member *of the human family*. No one can say he is not responsible for the well-being of his brother or sister (cf. Gen 4:9; Luke 10:29–37; Matt 25:31–46). (no. 51)

While affirming the right to private property, the famously anti-communist John Paul II nevertheless wrote that private property is not an absolute value in light of the universal destination of the earth's goods.[7] He proclaimed:

When there is question of defending the rights of individuals, the defenseless and the poor have a claim to special consideration. The richer class has many ways of shielding itself, and stands less in need of help from the State; whereas the mass of the poor have no resources of their own to fall back on, and must chiefly depend on the assistance of the State. It is for this reason that wage-earners, since they mostly belong to the latter class, should be specially cared for and protected by the Government. (no. 10)

What would John Paul II have thought of the Trump administration's many "deterrence" strategies, including separating children from their parents to dissuade other desperate people from coming to the border? It is not a stretch to suggest that he would have been aghast.

In *Centesimus Annus*, John Paul II emphasized, per Thomas Aquinas, the essentially social nature of every human. He saw that all of us can only become virtuous in the context of social groups, "beginning with the family, and including social, political and cultural groups, always with a view to the common good" (no. 13). He wrote that we must always be guided by "a comprehensive picture" of what constitutes a human person, "which respects all the dimensions of his being and which subordinates his material and instinctive dimensions to his interior and spiritual ones" (no. 36).

---

7. John Paul II, *Centesimus Annus*, no. 6 (emphasis added). Cf. encyclical letter *Rerum Novarum*, 102f.

Furthermore, he taught that amassing and protecting our own things and lifestyles at the expense of other people's dignity is wrong. Echoing Leo XIII a century earlier, John Paul II sounded a clarion-call warning against the danger in "advanced economies" of the phenomenon of consumerism, which he describes as "a style of life which is presumed to be better when it is directed towards 'having' rather than 'being,' and which wants to have more, not in order to be more but in order to spend life in enjoyment as an end in itself" (nos. 33–36).

Quoting Pope Leo before him, John Paul II warned starkly that although private property is legitimate, "those whom fortune favors are admonished . . . that they should tremble at the warnings of Jesus Christ . . . and that a most strict account must be given to the Supreme Judge for the use of all they possess." Quoting Aquinas, John Paul II continued, "But if the question be asked, how must one's possessions be used? The Church replies without hesitation that man should not consider his material possessions as his own, but as common to all" (no. 30).

He wrote that "God gave the earth to the whole human race for the sustenance of all its members, without excluding or favoring anyone" (no. 31). That the United States separated scared and suffering children from their parents as a deterrence strategy to keep them and other poor and suffering human beings from entering the country is contrary to everything that John Paul II taught. Moreover, John Paul II specifically taught that Catholics must always protect the family unit as the "sanctuary of life," writing that our natural human rights include "the right to live in a united family and in a moral environment conducive to the growth of the child's personality" (nos. 39, 47).

Veritatis Splendor

Just two years after *Centesimus Annus*, John Paul II released *Veritatis Splendor*, his masterful teaching on the "Catholic way" of resolving moral dilemmas. He framed the encyclical with the story of the rich young man who approaches Jesus in the Gospel of Matthew, asking, "Teacher, what good deed must I do to have eternal life?" (Matt 19:16). He noted that "no one can escape this fundamental question" (no. 2). John Paul II observed that the young man senses the "connection between moral good and the fulfillment of his own destiny." In other words, the young man recognizes that there is a deep connection between how we act and our own destinies. John Paul II concludes that drawing close to Christ is necessary to find the answer to the young man's question and that we owe the moral life to God, as our "response of love," due to the many gratuitous initiatives taken by God out of love for us (cf. no. 10).

To answer the young man's pressing question, John Paul II turned immediately to natural law:

> God has already given an answer to this question: he did so *by creating man and ordering him* with wisdom and love to his final end, through the law which is inscribed in his heart (cf. Rom 2:15), the "natural law." The latter "is nothing other than the light of understanding infused in us by God, whereby we understand what must be done and what must be avoided. God gave this light and this law to man at creation. (*Veritatis Splendor*, no. 12)

John Paul II wrote that the Ten Commandments, which reveal the natural law, were God's gift to us, and that their very foundation is the commandment of love of neighbor. He taught that inherent in the Ten Commandments are "*the need to protect human life*, the communion of persons in marriage, private property, truthfulness and peoples' good name" (nos. 12 and 13; emphasis added).

Turning to the question of *who* is our neighbor (see Luke 10:29), John Paul II didn't look to borders. Rather, he gave Jesus's response: the Samaritan (the historical enemy of the Jews) is the neighbor. He taught that unless we love the neighbor, who is a foreigner, or our enemy, we are not genuinely loving of God (see no. 14). He concluded, "Thus the commandment 'you shall not murder' becomes a call to an attentive love which *protects and promotes the life* of one's neighbor" (nos. 14, 15; emphasis added).

John Paul II repeatedly warned against overattachment to wealth, which often leads to the rejection of the "other," who becomes a threat. He wrote that "those who live 'by the flesh' experience God's law [love of neighbor] as a burden," while those who are "impelled by love and 'walk by the Spirit' (Gal 5:16), and who desire to serve others," find in God's law the way in which to practice love freely.[8] John Paul II taught that it was for this reason that Jesus advised the young man to give up his wealth and "come follow me" (Matt 19:21). John Paul II taught us to hold fast to the person of Jesus, not to wealth. Doing so means acting out of a love that gives itself completely to others (see nos. 19, 20).

Natural Law and the Common Good

John Paul II unambiguously proclaimed that natural law and the common good demand, above everything else, that we respect and preserve every person's life. He thus provided his list of "acts which *per se* and in themselves, independently of circumstances, *are always seriously wrong* by reason of their object," and *must always be avoided* in moral decision making:

> *Whatever is hostile to life itself,* such as any kind of homicide, genocide, abortion, euthanasia and voluntary suicide; *whatever violates the integrity of the human person,* such as mutilation, physical and mental torture and attempts to coerce the spirit; *whatever is offensive to human dignity,* such as subhuman living conditions, arbitrary imprisonment, deportation, slavery, prostitution and trafficking in women and children; degrading conditions of work which treat laborers as mere instruments of profit, and not as free responsible persons: all these and the like are a disgrace.... (no. 80; emphasis added)

Therefore, based on John Paul II's teaching in *Veritatis Splendor*, Catholics may not support, cooperate with, or look the other way from a government that is hostile or indifferent to *any* life, including migrant life, and that violates the integrity of migrating human persons, even if the cooperation or support is in the hope that some other perceived good will come from such support or cooperation. John Paul II made it clear: no step in the plan may be evil.

---

8. Cf. John Paul II, *Veritatis Splendor*, no. 18.

12

Pope Francis

Following the road map of John Paul II's clear teaching on immigration, Pope Francis's words and actions have continued to demonstrate that, for Catholics, welcoming the suffering stranger is not a secondary issue that is less important than other life issues. There are no life issues that are less important. Natural law and the Catholic way do not permit this kind of relativism. Opposing abortion but supporting the deportation of suffering people is clearly not Catholic. After the foundational natural law precept that good is to be done and evil avoided, the very next precept is that "whatever is a means of preserving human life and of warding off obstacles to life, belongs to the natural law."[1]

Exactly like John Paul II, Pope Francis's view of migrants comes directly from the natural law principle of the dignity of every human person, what a human person is and is for, and fundamentally what it means to be a Christian. In Francis's 2018 apostolic exhortation on holiness, *Gaudete et Exsultate*,[2] he made just this point:

> If I encounter a person sleeping outdoors on a cold night, I can view him or her as an annoyance, an idler, an obstacle in my path, a troubling sight, a problem for politicians to sort

---

1. Thomas Aquinas, *Summa Theologica*, Part II, I, Q. 94, "The Natural Law," Art. 2.

2. Pope Francis, apostolic exhortation *Gaudete et Exsultate* (Rejoice and Be Glad—"On the Call to Holiness in Today's World"), March 19, 2018, https://m.vatican.va.

out, or even a piece of refuse cluttering a public space. Or I
can respond with faith and charity, and see in this person a
human being with a dignity identical to my own, a creature
infinitely loved by the Father, an image of God, a brother or
sister redeemed by Jesus Christ. This is what it is to be a Christian! (no. 98)

Francis teaches with both words and gestures that it is part of the
DNA of what makes a person "Christian" to see and treat migrants,
and all "others" whom we fear, as fellow human beings, neighbors,
persons with equal dignity to our own, and brothers and sisters.

Francis speaks in a less formal style in the twenty-first century
than did predecessors, but his message is precisely the same. He
grounds every teaching in Scripture, from the admonishments in
the Hebrew Bible against oppressing the resident alien because "you
yourselves were strangers in the land of Egypt (Exod 22:21) to Jesus's
prophetic words in which he warns that if we do not recognize his
own face in the face of the stranger during our lifetimes, we will ultimately "go away into eternal punishment" (Matt 25:31–46).

Just like John Paul II, Francis has repeatedly warned against our
culture of indifference toward those who suffer. On July 8, 2013,
Francis chose as his very first trip as pope outside Rome to travel to
the Italian island of Lampedusa, a point of entry for refugees seeking
a way into Europe. In his homily during Mass, Francis challenged
the world to see all refugees as our neighbors, and indeed, our brothers and sisters. He pleaded with the whole world to have "a concrete
change of heart."[3]

Echoing John Paul II's warning in *Veritatis Splendor* against
"overattachment to wealth," which, as John Paul II says, often leads
to the rejection of the "other" as a threat and a burden, Francis
warned against what he called "the globalization of indifference":

The culture of comfort, which makes us think only of ourselves, makes us insensitive to the cries of other people, makes

---

3. Pope Francis, "Homily on the Island of Lampedusa," July 8, 2013, http://
m.vatican.va.

us live in soap bubbles which, however lovely, are insubstantial; they offer a fleeting and empty illusion that results in indifference to others; indeed it even leads to the globalization of indifference. . . . We have become used to the suffering of others: it doesn't affect me; it doesn't concern me; it's none of my business![4]

John Paul II could have written these words.

As we noted in the previous chapter, in *Centesimus Annus*, John Paul II affirmed the dogma of our Catholic faith that we *must* protect the transcendent dignity of every human person, in every situation. He taught that we have a "grave obligation" to ensure that life is preserved and that every person has the natural right to procure what is required to live. Furthermore, he taught that the defenseless and the poor, like the children and families in this book, have a claim to special consideration from us as Christians. He stated that "no one can consider himself extraneous or indifferent to the lot of another member of the human family."[5] In the very same way, Francis has taught consistently that, as followers of Jesus, we must preserve the lives of each and every immigrant person. He has repeatedly told us that these people are our brothers and sisters. And he has implored us to avoid the mindset of the "throwaway culture" that is a result of "the hardened heart of humanity."[6] In a 2015 address to diplomats from around the world, Francis implored:

Rejection is an attitude we all share; it makes us see our neighbor not as a brother or sister to be accepted but as unworthy of our attention, a rival, or someone to be bent to our will. This is the mindset that fosters a "throwaway culture" that spares nothing and no one—nature, human beings, even God himself. It gives rise to a humanity filled with pain and constantly torn by tensions and conflicts of every sort.

---

4. Ibid.

5. John Paul II, *Centesimus Annus*, nos. 6, 8, 10, 30–31.

6. Pope Francis, "Address to Members of the Diplomatic Corps Accredited to the Holy See," January 12, 2015, http://m.vatican.va.

Often coming without documents to strange lands whose language they do not speak, migrants find it difficult to be accepted and to find work. In addition to the uncertainties of their flight, they have to face the drama of rejection. A change of attitude is needed on our part, moving from indifference and fear to genuine acceptance of others.[7]

In more recent messages, Francis has become increasingly specific about what Catholics must do to "welcome the stranger." In his "Message for 2016, World Day of Migrants and Refugees," Francis reminded us that God's love "is particularly concerned for the needs of the sheep who are wounded, weary or ill." Francis boldly stated that we simply cannot look the other way, when millions of men, women, and children migrants are facing severe difficulties and even death. Francis stated plainly: "Indifference and silence lead to complicity."[8]

What must we do? In Francis's "Message for 2017, World Day of Migrants and Refugees," he wrote that, first, we must recognize that the phenomenon of migration is part of salvation history. The migration happening in the world now is a "sign of the times" and an opportunity *for us*. Like his predecessors, Francis taught that migrating people provide us with a precious opportunity to develop virtue, by grasping that each person is precious, that people—even strangers—are more important than things, and that our own worth will ultimately be measured by the way we treat others.[9] Thomas Aquinas would certainly agree! This is the Catholic way.

Francis teaches that, as Catholic Christians, we must all work concretely to protect every suffering person who migrates and to integrate each person into our society. Quoting a 2008 address by Pope Benedict, Francis advised that Catholics must "specifically

---

7. Ibid.

8. Pope Francis, "Message of His Holiness Pope Francis for the World Day of Migrants and Refugees 2016," January 17, 2016, https://m.vatican.va.

9. Pope Francis, "Message of His Holiness Pope Francis for the World Day of Migrants and Refugees 2017," January 15, 2017, http://m.vatican.va.

guarantee" the protection and safety of child migrants.[10] We may *never* turn a child away or lock him in a cage or a jail. We must cry with Gilberto and Liliana and Gabriela and Javi, and we must protect them until they can stand on their own.

Second, Francis says that each of us must work for the integration of migrant children and families into our communities. And finally, each of us must recognize that migration is driven by things outside of any individual family's control, like wars, human rights violations, corruption, poverty, environmental imbalance, and natural disasters. We must never demonize migrants with dehumanizing rhetoric. Instead, we must do our best to contribute to long-term solutions that deal with the causes that trigger migration in the first place.[11]

In full harmony with the teachings of John Paul II and his predecessors, Francis's key teaching begins with the direction to recognize migrants as our brothers and sisters, who are loved deeply by God. Migrants are not "invaders." Each person is our own concrete opportunity to encounter Jesus and be what we profess. We must welcome, protect, and integrate our new neighbors, while at the same time electing leaders who will promote the kind of justice that addresses the root causes of migration.

---

10. Ibid.
11. Ibid.

13

Doing What the Lord Asks

Often coming without documents to strange lands whose language they do not speak, migrants find it difficult to be accepted and to find work. In addition to the uncertainties of their flight, they have to face the drama of rejection. A change of attitude is needed on our part, moving from indifference and fear to genuine acceptance of others.

—Pope Francis, January 12, 2015

An unaccompanied child migrant will not likely be allowed to stay in the United States without a lawyer to navigate the immigration system. But it takes considerably much more than a lawyer for the children to be able to recover from trauma, adjust, and build a life in the United States. No child leaves their home, loved ones, and country alone, when everything is fine—on a lark.

Some unaccompanied children, like Gabriela, Javi, and Liliana, have suffered severe forms of abandonment, neglect, and abuse at the hands of a parent in their home countries. Others, like Gilberto and the Flores children, have experienced terrible persecution, including stalking, shootings, and murders of family members. Most of the arriving children do not speak English. Although some children reunite with a parent or family member in the United States, as Liliana's case readily demonstrates, the children's hopes and expectations of the parent seldom match the eventual reality.

Even if the child has a strong legal case for asylum or SIJS, the process can take several years. During that time, the child cannot get in trouble with the law, use drugs or alcohol, or drop out of school. Unless the child is exceptionally resilient, quickly recovers from trauma, and adjusts to attending a new school in a new country in a foreign language, the child is at significant risk of being sent back, regardless of having the lawyer.

Martha DeLira

There are numerous ways that nonlawyers can welcome and assist immigrant children and other suffering people as they make their way through the difficult process of gaining documented status. Lay men and women are doing this valuable service for migrant children across the country, in ways large and small. They donate clothing, furniture, and school supplies. They help the children enroll in school and find the right classes to meet their needs. They tutor. They locate counseling resources so that the children can deal with trauma, and sometimes they bring them to appointments. They take the children on outings, introduce them to their own families, and provide safe spaces for the children to play. What they offer is an open-hearted response to Jesus's command that Christians welcome the suffering stranger and take care of children. One woman who has been exemplary in welcoming children in Los Angeles is Martha DeLira. This is Martha's story.

In 2015, Martha was a sixty-six-year-old, recently retired Catholic woman, living in a suburb of Los Angeles. Martha is a long-time member of Resurrection Catholic Parish, where she attends Mass daily. She is devoted to Jesus and to the Blessed Mother. For many years, and long before she retired, Martha made periodic trips to Tijuana, Mexico, her car loaded with supplies and gifts for Casa del Migrante, a shelter for migrants run by the Scalabrini religious order, and for an orphanage for children run by a group of religious sisters.

Following the press attention in 2014 on the surge of unaccompanied children at the border, Martha responded to a call at Mass for bilingual volunteers to be trained by KIND to act as translators for pro bono lawyers helping these children in legal proceedings. Martha attended the KIND training for volunteer translators and has never looked back. Since 2014, Martha has translated for dozens of children and their lawyers as they made their way through the complicated immigration processes. But more importantly, Martha has befriended, accompanied, mentored, and assisted the children as they struggled to learn English and to adjust to their new lives.

Family Background

Martha was born in 1949 to her mother, Maria del Carmen, in Guadalajara, Mexico. Although Martha did not know it for many years, her mother, who went by "Carmen," had become pregnant as a result of rape. This brought great shame to her family, and the blame fell on young Maria. Even though it was not her fault, Carmen left town in shame and went to Los Angeles, where she got a job making tortillas in a restaurant.

Carmen left her baby with her parents in Guadalajara. Though furious at their daughter, the grandparents welcomed and were loving to their new granddaughter, Martha, who fondly recalls her grandfather's skillful violin playing, his warm smile, and apparent delight in her.

In Los Angeles, Carmen met a man called Raymundo DeLira. They fell in love and married. Raymundo had two young children, on whom he doted, from his first marriage. Raymundo encouraged Carmen to return to Guadalajara to retrieve her young daughter, Martha, and, in May 1955, helped her to do it. Her parents were shocked that she had found anyone who would marry her, much less take on her child. They brought six-year-old Martha to a new life in Los Angeles. Raymundo became Martha's true father, and Raymundo's sons, Richard and Steven, became her real brothers. Raymundo and Carmen had another son, Carlos, and two more daughters, Dolores and Sheila, who rounded out the DeLira family of Los Angeles.

Studies

Martha's parents enrolled her at the School of Santa Isabel, the same school that Carlos and Richard attended. In the 1950s, the children were taught by sisters in full habits. Martha spoke no English at the outset, but she learned quickly. She was the smart little girl who always had her hand up and, to the chagrin of the sisters, would sometimes shout out the answer when she was not called on. The sisters helped Martha to overcome this problem by moving her up a grade (and telling her to stop). Many years later, she remains a bright and confident woman. In 2017, Martha proudly sat in the audience watching a young unaccompanied Guatemalan boy whom she had mentored graduate from eighth grade at Santa Isabel School, which he had attended on scholarship.

Martha attended high school in the mid-1960s at Bishop Conaty High School, a Catholic girls' school in central Los Angeles, run by sisters from six different religious orders. Martha had to take two buses to get to the school from her family's home in East L.A. Martha's family did not have much money, and attending a Catholic high school was expensive. Martha was able to attend Bishop Conaty High School by working during the school year through the high school's partnership with the Neighborhood Youth Corps, a program launched by President Lyndon Johnson in 1964 as part of his "Great Society" and its war on poverty.

At first, Martha did filing in the school office before the school day started. Her next job was serving meals in the school cafeteria. Eventually, the cafeteria staff realized that Martha could do the sums to calculate the prices for the meals in her head, and she became the cafeteria cashier. Martha had always loved math and science. She studied hard and worked to pay for her tuition. Martha graduated from Bishop Conaty with top grades in 1967.

Even as a young child, Martha had imagined working in a laboratory. After high school, she enrolled at the Southland College of Medical, Dental and Legal Careers to learn how to be a medical assistant. When she completed her studies, a neurologist and family practitioner named Dr. Horacio Ariza hired Martha to help him start up his new medical practice. Very soon, Martha was running the practice and acting as Dr. Ariza's nurse. She worked with Dr. Ariza, a lifelong friend, for thirteen years. Martha was Dr. Ariza's right-hand person. Over the years, Martha enhanced her skills by obtaining certifications as an X-ray technician and phlebotomist.

Motherhood

In 1982, when she was thirty-three years old, Martha's life changed in a way she had never imagined. Her brother Carlos had befriended a single woman called Evangeline, who was pregnant with twins. Carlos tried to encourage Evangeline, who had confided in him that she did not think she could keep the babies. Evangeline carried the babies to term, but when they arrived, one was stillborn. Evangeline briefly tried to keep the surviving baby but quickly realized she could not cope. Carlos brought the infant, called Esteban, or Stevie, home, suggesting that Martha should adopt him.

Martha was stunned. She had recently lost the love of her life, whom she had thought she would marry. Her work kept her very busy, and she did not see herself becoming a single mother. But Martha prayed, and she listened to her heart and to her mother, Carmen, who told her, "Mija, that baby may grow up to be your companion."

Martha became Stevie's mom. Stevie, as a baby, was colicky, so Martha would sit up with him night after night, rocking him and feeding him bottles. She spoke Spanish to Stevie, knowing he would learn English in school. Like Martha, Stevie is now bilingual. Martha sent Stevie to a private kindergarten and then to Resurrection Catholic School in East L.A. After that, Stevie attended Bishop Mora Salesian High School, an all-male Catholic school. Stevie is a hard worker, who attended Santa Monica City College and now works as the information technology manager of a law firm. For many years, Stevie has accompanied Martha on her trips to Tijuana to bring supplies to struggling immigrants. He has, in fact, been a real companion to Martha.

While Martha was working for Dr. Ariza, her father, Raymundo, became ill with a tumor and congestive heart failure. Martha realized that Raymundo was not receiving attentive care from his HMO. She loved Raymundo dearly and was deeply grateful to him, not only for being a father to her but also for encouraging her mother to return to Mexico and bring her to the United States. When the HMO refused to provide the right care for Raymundo, Martha paid for Raymundo's treatment at Cedars Sinai Medical Center. Raymundo DeLira died in 1987 at age 103. Martha's beloved mother, Carmen, died four years later.

Career

In 1984, Martha left Dr. Ariza to take a position as team leader in the phlebotomy department at UCLA Hospital. There, she led teams of phlebotomists who daily drew blood from patients in the large hospital system. She taught nurses to draw blood, lectured on blood issues, and worked with the special blood-related needs of the oncology department. After ten years at UCLA, Martha took a similar position at Children's Hospital Los Angeles, where she drew blood from the tiniest infants in the neonatal intensive care unit, blessing them and praying for the very sick babies as she worked. At Children's Hospital, Martha trained others in drawing blood and in processing the blood specimens as well. At the same time, Martha worked at Cedars Sinai Medical Center to support her family. Martha returned to UCLA Medical Center in 2006 and worked there until she retired.

Martha's scrapbooks are full of letters of commendation and personal notes of gratitude from the doctors, nurses, and patients at all three of these hospitals. Most of these notes comment on her warm, friendly manner and her ability to make young patients and their parents feel comfortable in the most difficult circumstances. Others comment that due to her sensitivity, diplomacy, and conscientiousness, things worked just the way they should when Martha was around. One commendation noted her conscientious and dedicated service during the L.A. Riots of 1992, when many employees simply didn't go to work.

When Martha's friend Dr. Ariza retired, he sold his medical practice to Dr. Manuel Saenz. As she does with everyone, Martha forged a friendship with Dr. Saenz as well. Dr. Saenz is a "civil surgeon," which means he is approved by USCIS to perform the specialized medical examinations that are required for anyone who applies to become a green card holder. Based on this long friendship, Martha now helps many children to get their medical examination at reduced cost.

Ministry

Over the years, Martha has been part of many ministries at Resurrection Parish, including working in the church's bookstore and maintaining its St. Francis garden. Asked why she responded to the 2015 call for volunteers to translate for and mentor unaccompanied children, Martha said her mother's lifelong example compelled her to act. She said that her mother, Carmen, herself an immigrant, always helped the immigrant stranger:

> My mom helped anyone who asked. She told me and she showed me to help anyone who is hungry or thirsty. When I was young, and a migrant knocked on our door, my mom always gave them dinner and a thermos of coffee. Now, these kids are knocking at the door of my heart. I have enough. I have everything I need—a place to live and friends.
>
> I have our Lord and his Blessed Mother. I see that it takes tremendous courage for the people who are coming to this country, just to get through each day, just hoping for a chance to have their dreams become reality. I know my mom is proud of me.
>
> I just do what the Lord asks.

The first child Martha took on—a boy called Jose from El Salvador—came to the United States after learning that his father, who worked at a car wash in Long Beach, had died of a heart attack at age thirty-seven. Jose's mother disappeared while trying to make her way to Los Angeles to bury her husband. When Jose was released from the ORR detention facility, he moved in with an aunt who lived in the country as a Temporary Protected Status (TPS) beneficiary. Jose's aunt welcomed him, but she did not speak English and could not help Jose navigate the immigration system or the large public high school he needed to attend. Jose had simply accepted the computer-generated schedule he was handed when he enrolled himself.

When Martha learned that Jose was floundering in school, she went to the school with Jose. Together, they learned what the school had to offer. Martha helped Jose to get a school counselor and to choose courses appropriate to his situation. Jose began to learn English and soon began to thrive. His school took an interest in him, thanks to Martha's intervention, and he eventually played varsity soccer, with Martha cheering in the stands. Jose graduated from high school and now has a stable life and a good job. He obtained his green card in 2018.

Since working with Jose, Martha has helped dozens of other children—like Gabriela and Javi, and many others. She has attended their court hearings for moral support (even when translation is not required), accompanied children to interviews by social workers, translated at asylum hearings, intervened in abuse situations, attended school events and graduations, arranged tutoring and medical care, and has been, in general, a calm, loving friend to our newest neighbors. Martha lives the teaching of Pope Francis every day.

14

Comprehensive Immigration Reform—A Catholic Proposal

Most Americans will readily agree that the U.S. immigration system is broken and that our laws need to be changed. At the same time, most people—even most lawyers who don't practice immigration law—do not actually understand existing immigration law and system.

Immigration law is federal—applying uniformly across all the states—which means that Congress created the law and is responsible for any changes to it.[1] No president can change immigration law. However, the U.S. Congress has been unable to reach agreement on how to change immigration law through successive presidential administrations.

Bypassing Congress: The DACA and DAPA Programs

Out of frustration at Congress's inability or refusal to address the situation, Mr. Obama bypassed Congress when he created the Deferred Action for Childhood Arrivals (DACA) program and the

---

1. One exception to what Congress can change by the ordinary process of passing laws (by majority vote in House and Senate and signature by the president) is so-called birthright citizenship. The concept that all persons born in the United States are citizens is found in the Fourteenth Amendment to the U.S. Constitution, adopted in 1868. The Constitution can only be changed by a two-thirds majority vote by both the House and the Senate or by a constitutional convention called for by two-thirds of the states' legislatures. The president cannot change the Constitution.

Deferred Action for Parents of Americans (DAPA) program that followed it in 2014. DACA, which is discussed at greater length in Appendix II, gave temporary permission to work and a two-year deferral of deportation—subject to discretionary renewal—to young people brought to the United States by their parents when they were children. DAPA, a program that never went into effect, was similarly aimed at deferring the deportation of undocumented parents of citizens or green card holders.

Mr. Obama authorized DACA and DAPA with the stroke of a pen, when Congress failed to reform immigration law. Neither of these programs was "law" passed by Congress. Mr. Obama admitted that he was acting on his own, without Congress, to try to fix as much of the immigration system as he could. In the long run, this bypass-Congress approach does not work in this country. DAPA was stopped by the federal courts as having exceeded the president's power. Mr. Trump unilaterally ended DACA, though court challenges continue on the question of whether the Trump administration complied with the law in the manner of the termination. The long-term viability of DACA is highly doubtful.

The Trump administration, like its predecessors, has been unable to persuade Congress to change immigration law. Using precisely the same strategy as did the Obama administration, but on an exponentially greater scale, the Trump administration, in frustration, has announced a series of policy changes described not as new laws but rather as changes to how the existing immigration law is implemented. These policy changes have been single-mindedly focused on two goals: reducing immigration of all but highly educated people from the "right parts" of the world, and ending all forms of humanitarian relief that are available to the suffering poor. Most of the policy changes announced by the Trump administration have been challenged in the federal courts and halted, similar to Mr. Obama's DAPA policy.

Current Law and Policies

Before considering a Catholic faith-informed reform of U.S. immigration law that Catholics could encourage Congress to enact, it is essential to have at least a basic grasp of what law and policies exist. A more fulsome summary of current immigration law and the immigration system is contained in the appendix to this book. In summary, here are four points to remember when considering reform:

1. Under current law, it is exceedingly difficult *for anyone* to gain permission to migrate to live and work long-term in the United States as a permanent resident. There are only four roads:

Family-based migration, which some people derogatorily call "chain migration," allows U.S. citizens and green card holders to sponsor a relative to migrate to the United States. This road is limited to 480,000 people per year. Because of this numerical limitation, family-based migration is extremely slow, and some people wait decades for their relative's turn. Family-based migration does not help children or any suffering people escaping from real-time threats to life.

Employment-based migration is even more limited—to 140,000 persons per year. Employment-based migration is available (on other than a nonimmigrant, temporary basis) only to professionals and other highly skilled persons through a corporate sponsor, who can prove that no one already in the country can do the job.

The *Diversity Lottery*, a program started in the 1980s, allows a small number of people (50,000 persons per year) to migrate from countries with low representation in the United States. The program is small. It certainly does not provide a way out of real-time persecution and suffering for anyone.

Humanitarian relief, contrary to what most people believe, is granted in very few cases. Suffering people, whom this country acknowledges have fled from terrible persecution and life-and-death situations, are routinely turned away because their proven persecution is not the "right kind."

Each of the four "roads" to legal migration comes with the ability to apply for lawful permanent resident (LPR/green card) status within a specified period of time. Once a person has a green card, they may apply for citizenship in five years.

2. The United States simply does not allow most of the suffering people in the world—even those trying to save their lives—to enter, reside, and work lawfully in the country. This was true before the Trump administration. Since Mr. Trump's election, it has gotten much worse. Before 2017, this country accepted a small fraction of such people, and only when they proved that they faced severe persecution that was because of their race, religion, national origin, political opinion, or membership in a particular social group. People who are desperate to save their lives and those of their families—but whose persecution does not fit squarely into one of the five categories—may have no practical choice but to enter the country through the "back door" (not at a legal border crossing), to live and work in the country at constant risk of being caught and deported.

3. Defenses to being deported for people who are caught in the United States without permission exist for only a few, very narrow categories of people who experienced child abuse, sexual abuse, trafficking, or were victims of serious crimes in the United States. The number of people who can obtain these exceptions to being deported is strictly limited, and the procedures to apply are complicated. Practically, most of ten to twelve million undocumented people in the United States today have no defense under the law to being deported.

4. United States immigration law, like tax law, is complex, and its administration is decentralized across the federal government. The process favors affluent people who can pay lawyers to navigate for them. The process is exceptionally challenging for poor and suffering migrants, who are not entitled to a free lawyer even when they are held in detention. They are unlikely to know how and where to prepare and present a case.

A Catholic Response

There is no single "Catholic" response to all migration situations. The faith requires no particular position on people who are living safely, with their families, with adequate resources in their home countries. Catholics are free to consult their own informed consciences when evaluating proposals to regulate the admission of such people to the country. Nor does Catholic teaching preclude border security, for the common good, protecting all people from criminal and terroristic acts.

As we must do when evaluating any human-created law, Catholics must always keep in mind that human laws must be for the common good. In other words, we must recognize that all humans are social creatures with a God-given need to live in society with other people. We must seek laws that enable all people in the world to live safely, and to find God. *Everyone* is included in this common good. It is *not* limited to people living on one side of the border.

Where no "life" issues are implicated, Catholic people educated in our laws and system may reasonably arrive at different conclusions. However, when people come to the country in fear for their lives or are unable to survive in their home countries for any reason, a life issue is presented. Catholics must support reform to U.S. immigration law that is consistent with the first principle of natural law: *to preserve life*. In the words of Pope St. John Paul II, Catholics of any political stripe may support *only* immigration reform that eliminates "whatever is hostile to life itself ... whatever violates the integrity of the human person ... whatever is offensive to human dignity, such as subhuman living conditions, arbitrary imprisonment, deportation, slavery, prostitution and trafficking in women and children" (*Veritatis Splendor*, no. 80).

It is for these reasons that the United States Conference of Catholic Bishops (USCCB) teaches American Catholics to follow the gospel mandate to "welcome the stranger," which quite specifically means always to "care for and stand with newcomers authorized and unauthorized." The bishops expressly direct Catholics to care for unaccompanied immigrant children, like Gilberto, Gabriela, Javi, and Liliana, and asylum seekers, like the Flores family. The bishops expressly support allowing newly arrived migrants to work as they go through the immigration process, and always to have access to legal protections. The bishops decry the use of detention of migrants as a deterrent to others who are fleeing for their lives.[2] Life issues are

---

2. United States Conference of Catholic Bishops, *Forming Consciences for*

life issues. Catholics may not oppose abortion and ignore suffering migrants.

Foundational Precepts

Here are the foundational precepts that must underlie any reform of U.S. immigration law that Catholics can support:

1. The periodic need of humans to migrate is part of the natural law. This periodic need must be acknowledged and respected as part of what it means to be human.

2. Every human person, including migrating persons, must be respected and their dignity preserved in every situation. This is true, no matter how many people ask for help.

3. Human lives—no matter where people are from, their race, color, or their creed—cannot be weighed or balanced against others, so the "greatest number" (or people already in a country) get the "greatest good," protect their possessions, or safeguard their culture or standard of living. All humans, on any side of a border, rich or poor, of any race or creed, are our brothers and sisters.

4. Every human life in jeopardy, for any reason, must be preserved. This is regardless of whether a migrant is "authorized or unauthorized" to enter the country. Catholics may never support laws that permit deporting people to places where they risk death or where they cannot sustain themselves and their families with dignity.

5. Every child who asks for help must be welcomed, cared for, fed, educated, and nurtured. Every child! Children may never be demonized as "invaders" or "wolves in sheep's clothing." The "best interest of the child" must be placed at the center of the immigration law.

6. Children must be allowed to live with their families unless, for an unusual reason, it is not in the child's best interest. Protecting the family, the heart of natural law, is a paramount virtue.

Faithful Citizenship: A Call to Political Responsibility from the Catholic Bishops of the United States with Introductory Note, no. 81, November 2015, www.usccb.org.

7. If a human law, such as the current U.S. law under which people are routinely deported to face danger, violates the natural law, then it is "no law at all." Just as Catholics do not take, or tacitly support taking, the lives of the unborn, we may never condone, participate in, support, or look the other way when U.S. law leads to loss of life or the separation of children from their families.

Specific Reforms

These precepts, drawn from natural law and the consistent teaching of the church, lead to the following specific reforms to U.S. law and policy, all of which can be implemented by Congress:

1. United States asylum law must be changed to be available to all persecuted people. Current law, which limits asylum to people who can prove that their persecutors acted "because of" the applicant's race, religion, national origin, political opinion, or social group, leads directly to loss of life and is contrary to natural law.
2. Applicants for asylum or other humanitarian relief must be allowed to work to support themselves and their families while their cases are being considered. Current U.S. policy, which restricts employment to deter migrants from coming to the United States, must be changed.
3. The numerical limitation on family-based migration (480,000 people per year) should be re-evaluated to take into account the public wealth of the United States, decreasing birth rates, anticipated future needs for workers, and the common good of all God's people. As Pope Pius XII stated in *Exsul Familia*, and contrary to the position of the Trump administration as announced by former ambassador Nikki Haley, the sovereignty of the United States "cannot be exaggerated to the point that access to this land is, for inadequate or unjustified reasons, denied to needy and decent people from other lands, provided of course, that the public wealth, considered very carefully, does not forbid this."
4. All four of the "roads" to live and work in the United States, and which come with the right to apply for a green card (LPR)—employment, family, Diversity Lottery, and humanitarian—

should be disconnected from an automatic right to apply for citizenship five years after obtaining LPR status. Our faith requires that we fully welcome the stranger. We must do so. But granting to some people but not others a right to apply for citizenship in five years has created strong disincentives to the required full and complete welcome. The current link in the law between initial admission (on one of the four roads) and citizenship has made it more difficult for suffering people to get the welcome they deserve. United States law should be changed so that each of the four roads includes a period of "provisional admission"—a probationary period during which the migrant demonstrates sustained ability to comply with the law and live peacefully in society—followed by the right to apply for LPR status.

5. Migrants must be good guests, meaning they must comply with the law and be respectful of the culture, which, by law, includes freedom of religion and freedom of speech, along with obligations such as paying taxes. But current U.S. law must also be changed so that "Lawful Permanent Resident" status means what it says. LPR status should be changed so that LPRs no longer live (as they presently do) under the perpetual threat of being deported for even relatively minor violations of the law. Deportation should no longer be used to punish LPRs who violate the law. Instead, LPRs should be subject to the same civil and criminal penalties as anyone else.

6. The immigration process should end when a person obtains LPR status or another permanent status that could be created to normalize persons who are presently living in the country without permission.

Following a lengthy period of discernment and discussion, the citizens of this country and their elected representatives should decide what any person who becomes an LPR must demonstrate, and for how long, before becoming a naturalized citizen. Americans have never had this discussion, although tacit agendas about who should and should not be allowed to gain citizenship bubble underneath the current administration's xenophobic, anti-immigrant rhetoric and restrictive policies. The

Trump administration claims to be taking citizenship seriously in its immigration policies. In reality, the administration is doing everything it can to keep people from non-European countries from becoming citizens. The citizenship question separated from the welcome we must offer to suffering migrants must be considered openly.

Obviously, consistent with the U.S. Constitution, the criteria ultimately chosen for migrants to become citizens can never be the applicant's race, color, religion or creed, sex, age, or physical or mental disability, as that would be against the law. As Catholics, we certainly could not base eligibility for citizenship on perceived superiority of some kinds of people—or their races or jobs—over others, given our belief that all humans have equal dignity. Nor would that be consistent with Thomas Jefferson's statement in the Declaration of Independence that "all men are created equal."

The American people must decide what any person who has migrated to this country and gained LPR status needs to demonstrate to become a citizen. The answer must apply to all migrants, rich or poor, of any race or creed, and regardless of whether the migrant initially came with an employment or family sponsor, through the Diversity Lottery, or through a form of humanitarian relief.

7. "Open borders" is not an objective of Catholic immigration reform. Countries may control their borders and maintain the rule of law for the common good, as that term is understood in Catholic thought. Requiring entrants to use only legal ports of entry and screening all who ask to enter a country to ensure they are being truthful about their need and to intercept dangerous criminals, drug and human traffickers, and terrorists are legitimate for the common good. At the same time, border security may not be abused. As Pope Pius XII proclaimed in *Exsul Familia*, a country's sovereignty "cannot be exaggerated to the point that access to the country is, for inadequate or unjustified reasons, denied to needy and decent people from other lands, provided of course, that the public wealth, considered very carefully, does not forbid this."

8. A process of "normalization" must be designed and implemented so that the ten to twelve million undocumented people living in the country may emerge from living in the shadows to living safely in society. The normalization process must preserve life in all cases and protect the family. People whose lives would be in danger in their home countries must never be deported, even if they violated the law when entering the country and the time limit for applying for asylum or other humanitarian relief has long expired. Children must never again be torn from parents.

   The normalization process must include the ability to work and live safely in society, though it could also include consequences, such as fines, penalties, and payment of back taxes for those who entered and worked in the country without permission. The normalization process for people who entered the country without permission does not necessarily have to include the possibility of becoming a citizen. Nevertheless, such persons must be treated with dignity and compassion.

9. DACA and Temporary Protected Status (TPS). These programs, for different reasons, were badly conceived from their inception. Just as Mr. Trump's various unilateral policy pronouncements that sidestepped Congress were poorly conceived and many halted by the courts, Mr. Obama's unilateral creation of DACA was a mistake. DACA was created in purported sympathy for the thousands of children living in the country who had no capacity to make decisions when they came and now have no relationship with their home countries. However, in bypassing Congress and announcing a "policy," Mr. Obama created a road map for Mr. Trump to do the same thing. Moreover, bypassing Congress created hostility toward the DACA program and a general understanding that its recipients are illegitimate. Furthermore, by portraying DACA recipients as "blameless" and "good," the program tacitly implied that their parents—many of whom may have been running for their lives or seeking a way to feed the children—are blameworthy and bad. DACA ultimately set back the cause of finding a comprehensive reform that includes all undocumented people.

Most important, DACA created no real solution for its recipients. Young DACA recipients believed the program was a first step toward becoming fully documented. It never was. Recipients proudly labeled themselves "DACAmented," believing that their situations had begun to be normalized. The use of an acronym, instead of the program's full name, subtly kept recipients from focusing on what it really was: signing up to be deported after a two-year delay, with the *possibility* for further delays that would be entirely at the discretion of the next administration. Mr. Trump's administration was not interested in further deferrals.

Nor was TPS—or at least its implementation—wise in hindsight. Unlike DACA, TPS was created by Congress, but it was conceived by Congress to provide *brief* periods of assistance to people in crisis. Congress authorized the federal government to give brief (six to eighteen months) respites in this country to people whose homelands had suffered sudden emergency situations that left them temporarily unable to safeguard their citizens. Beneficiaries of TPS were told from the beginning that they were not immigrants and that they could stay and work in the country only for the short term. But multiple administrations of both parties repeatedly extended TPS, allowing beneficiaries from some countries to remain in the United States for decades. TPS recipients did what people do: they formed families, had children, bought homes, held jobs, and contributed to their communities, all without any long-term security. Although beneficiaries knew there was a risk that TPS would end and they would be sent home, expectations grew with every extension—that they would continue to be allowed to stay. In light of this history, the Trump administration's pronouncements that TPS was ending for various countries and that people who had been allowed to stay in the country for decades must suddenly leave, though technically within the law, were cruel. Moreover, they served no purpose other than to pander to anti-immigrant, nationalist sentiment.

Both DACA and TPS—one a policy and the other a law— should be discontinued as part of immigration reform. But unlike the approach taken by the Trump administration, which would tear people away from their children, lives, and communities, TPS beneficiaries and DACA recipients must be given an opportunity to normalize their situations so that they can live in this country openly, subject to the rule of law. The normalization process must be based on the principles of preserving life in all cases and protecting the family. It must also include the ability to work and live safely in society, though it could also include fines, penalties, and the payment of back taxes. The normalization process does not necessarily include future eligibility to become a citizen.

Appendix I

Citizenship

What is the big deal about citizenship? Why should the citizenship process be disconnected from the immigration process? What does citizenship mean in a country like the United States that was founded by people from other places and largely populated by streams of immigrants and their descendants? Does it make any sense for some people to be deemed "citizenship eligible" when they first enter the country, and others not?

Existing U.S. immigration law separates people who wish to enter, live, and work in this country into "immigrant" and "nonimmigrant" boxes. Only the people in the four categories already discussed—sponsored by an employer, a family member, Diversity Lottery, or humanitarian relief—are in the immigrant box, deemed worthy to apply for LPR status and, after five years, citizenship. Other people who come to live and work in the United States are categorized at the outset as nonimmigrants. They can never become LPRs or citizens. Nonimmigrants are our seasonal agricultural workers. They are hospitality workers, cleaning hotel rooms and working in the restaurants at private clubs in Florida. They are nurses, reporters, "fashion models of distinguished merit and ability"—the actual language in the law—athletes, and entertainers. These so-called temporary nonimmigrants are allowed to come into the country for specified periods, but they are required to leave the country at the end of that period.

Nevertheless, there is a loophole for some nonimmigrants. In some cases, nonimmigrant artists, athletes, and people in certain professions—like the distinguished fashion models—are allowed to get green cards and become citizens, even though they entered the country as nonimmigrants. The nurses and the agricultural and hospitality workers never have this possibility. Why should this be? What possible purpose does it serve? Does a person's job indicate they would be a good citizen? Do distinguished fashion models make better citizens than cooks? Do distinguished fashion models make better citizens than ordinary fashion models? Are all people our brothers and sisters, of equal dignity, or do we actually believe that some people are better than others?

United States immigration law offers the possibility of becoming a U.S. citizen to all asylum recipients five years after they are awarded asylum. In other words, a person can become a citizen five years after proving that they endured the right kind of severe persecution (motivated by race, religion, national origin, political opinion, or social group) in their home countries. Other people who suffered the wrong kind of persecution (motivated by some other kind of animus) are not granted asylum, so cannot become citizens. Does suffering past persecution demonstrate that a person would be a good U.S. citizen? Does the reason one was persecuted have anything to do with whether a person should become a citizen?

Current U.S. law, which offers entry tied to the possibility of citizenship to some people because they were persecuted and to others for their employment skills or a family relationship but not to hardworking and diligent farm laborers or nurses makes no sense. What are our country's values here? What is it about fashion models and farm laborers that suggests the former make good citizens but the latter never do?

Separating the warm welcome we are compelled to offer to every suffering stranger from the political question of "who eventually gets to be a citizen" is necessary to open the door to all who have a natural law need to migrate. Separating the two concepts—welcome and citizenship—compels the country to look carefully at what we value and at what should be required for anyone to belong here. Following are some very basic considerations for discussion, as we discern together what it means to be citizens of the United States and what newcomers should be asked to demonstrate in order to apply to be one of us.

As Catholic Christians, we are all first and foremost citizens of God's world. Terms like "globalization" and "cosmopolitan citizenship" have been turned into negative buzzwords in the nationalism of the Trump era. This is not the Catholic way, as Pius XII warned. Jesus repeatedly taught us that we are all brothers and sisters. We are not separate from other people by virtue of borders. The Catholic faith never pretends that the lives of some people, from some places, come first.

The idea of citizenship in the twenty-first century has actually been studied extensively. Many scholarly volumes exist on what citizenship means and what it might mean. Since the 1990s, the field of citizenship studies has existed within the fields of history, political science, and the social sciences. We must take advantage of this scholarship.

From history, and also from the Bible, we learn that people have always migrated in times of need. Historically, "citizenship" was a status granted by the state to a subset of people who lived in a society, with rights and responsibilities conferred solely on the small group. This was the case in biblical times. For example, Paul surprises a group of centurions who are intent on whipping him by telling them that they cannot do so because he was a citizen of Rome, which conferred on him certain rights that not everyone had (see Acts 22:25–29). In those days, many people were not citizens anywhere. Should this be the case?

From sociology, we learn that, today, citizenship is about *belonging somewhere*. In a "diverse, unequal, and connected" world, we have come to assume that everyone belongs in a territorially defined state.[1] We tacitly assume that everyone is a citizen somewhere; some people believe that people should stay in their assigned places. Based on these assumptions, some Americans resist foreigners, who

---

1. Frederick Cooper, *Citizenship, Inequality, and Difference: Historical Perspectives* (Princeton, NJ: Princeton University Press, 2018), 4.

threaten to dilute them by taking rights regarded as not theirs to take. Is this what Jesus teaches?

Citizenship, today, has been called the "right to claim rights" in a specific place.[2] Consequently, the benefits of American citizenship include civil rights (free speech, freedom of movement, the rule of law), political rights (voting, seeking election), and social rights (social security, welfare, unemployment insurance, health care).[3] Are some people more deserving of these rights than others? Can a Catholic ever justify such a position? No. The problem with the modern concept of citizenship for Catholic Christians is that citizenship today generally means "a community that is smaller than humanity" (Americans vs. everyone else) and which directs the community's members "to serve each other and themselves preferentially over others."[4] But America first is not Jesus's way.

Today, most scholars agree that citizenship is composed of three main elements: a legal status, a political agency (the ability to act), and membership in a community with an identity.[5] Therefore, citizenship is not only a status but also a practice and an identity. How should a person be required to act to show they should be granted citizenship today? Who should be allowed to demand things or to vote for things in this country?

What is the identity of an American citizen today? What are the responsibilities of U.S. citizenship? Everyone knows that American citizens over eighteen years old have the right to vote. Doesn't citizenship also mean one has a responsibility to vote? Americans don't seem to think so. Voter turnout in the U.S. 2018 mid-term elections was considered high, even though only 36 percent of those eighteen-to twenty-nine-year-old citizens eligible to vote actually did so. (In fact, this was a considerable increase over the 2014 mid-term elections, in which only 20 percent of eighteen- to twenty-nine-year-

---

2. Cooper, *Citizenship,* 10.

3. Hein-Anton van der Heijden, ed., *Handbook of Political Citizenship and Social Movements* (Cheltenham, UK: Edward Elgar Publishing, 2014), 2.

4. Cooper, *Citizenship,* 143.

5. Van der Heijden, *Handbook of Political Citizenship,* 9–10.

old citizens voted.)[6] Overall, only half of the eligible citizens in this country voted in the 2018 mid-term elections (53 percent). And this was the highest voter turnout in a midterm election in forty years. Must an aspirant to citizenship demonstrate a willingness to participate in the democratic process to become a citizen, when existing citizens do not do so? Is citizen participation a defining element of American democracy? Twenty-two countries, including Australia, have mandatory voting. Should this country require that its citizens vote in elections as part of the duties of citizenship?

What are the characteristics that an aspiring citizen should demonstrate? Community involvement? Patriotic attitudes? Military service? A record of paying taxes? Charity work? Religious attendance? The Trump administration has attempted to implement a policy that using public benefits disqualifies an aspirant from ever becoming a citizen. Why?

There is much to discuss. Educated Catholics have much to add to the discussion. Hearts must change so that together we can offer the kind of welcome our suffering brothers and sisters desperately need and, for our own salvation, we need to offer.

---

6. Jordan Misra, "Voter Turnout Rates among All Voting Age and Major Racial and Ethnic Groups Were Higher Than in 2014," United States Census Bureau, April 23, 2019, https://www.census.gov.

Paul M. Holsinger

WOUNDED WARRIOR PROJECT®

Holly Ordway: Not God's Type

Edward Sri

Karl Keating: What Catholics Really Believe

Thomas Howard

Helen Walker Homan

Catherine Beebe

The Miracle of Our Lady of Fatima

The 13th Day

Fatima

U.S. Immigration Law and the Immigration System

United States immigration law is dense, and the system is seemingly impenetrable to the nonspecialist. The administration of immigration matters is spread across a number of federal agencies, with no single agency in charge. Each agency houses its own databases, and the agencies communicate poorly with one another.[1] The main federal agencies involved in immigration in the United States are:

1. *U.S. Citizenship and Immigration Services* (USCIS), a part of the Department of Homeland Security (DHS), is an entity created by Congress in 2003 in the wake of the 2001 terrorist attacks. Among other things, USCIS is involved in the selection of immigrants, the adjudication of eligibility for asylum (for some immigrants), work permits, and naturalization.
2. *Customs and Border Protection* (CBP) is also a part of DHS. CBP is responsible for protecting the border—including inspections, expedited removals (immediate deportation upon apprehension, without further due process), and border surveillance.
3. *Immigration and Customs Enforcement* (ICE) is another agency under DHS. ICE is responsible for the enforcement of the law within the country, including apprehension of undocumented persons, workplace raids, detention, processing, and deportations.

---

1. Ruth Ellen Wasem, "Immigration Governance for the Twenty-First Century," *Journal on Migration and Human Security* 6, no. 1 (2018): 105–6.

4. *Executive Office for Immigration Review* (EOIR) is the federal administrative court system for immigration. It is part of the U.S. Department of Justice (DOJ), not the DHS. EOIR judges decide outcomes for those people—both detained and nondetained—who are in removal proceedings, including those with asylum claims and appeals.

5. *Department of State* (DOS) and its *Bureau of Consular Affairs* (BCA) are responsible for the Diversity Lottery, admissibility to the country (from consulates), the consular "lookout and support system" for national security, and determining refugee priorities and the resettlement of those who attain "refugee" status.[2]

Additional federal agencies involved in the administration of immigration include the Centers for Disease Control and Prevention (CDC), the Department of Health and Human Services (HHS) and its Office of Refugee Resettlement (ORR), the Department of Labor, and others. As discussed in chapter 4 ("Gabriela and Javi's Story") and chapter 7 ("Liliana's Story"), child migrants who seek Special Immigrant Juvenile Status must also navigate the various state court systems. It is the rare immigrant who can navigate any of these agencies without an experienced lawyer.

The Four Roads to Citizenship

Many people vaguely assume that "anyone whose life is really in danger gets humanitarian relief." Others assume that people with special skills always get to come to the United States. Still other people claim that our immigration laws are so "full of holes that anyone can find a way in." None of these things are true. There are four main groups of people who may migrate to the United States to live and work, with a pathway to becoming a lawful permanent resident (LPR) and, in five years, a naturalized citizen. They are:

1. *Employment-Based Immigration.* United States employers can sponsor foreign-born employees for lawful permanent residence.

---

2. Wasem, "Immigration Governance," 106.

People who have been LPRs for five years may apply for citizenship. In most cases, to sponsor an employee as an LPR, the employer must first demonstrate to the Department of Labor that there is no qualified U.S. citizen available for the job, a process that requires documenting the employer's diligent, but unsuccessful, attempt to find a qualified U.S. worker who is willing and able to perform the job. The process is cumbersome. It is not something that most employers pursue casually. Employment-based immigration is strictly limited under U.S. law to 140,000 persons per year. This means that when 140,000 employment-based visas have been issued by USCIS in any year, no more are granted. A total of 140,000 people constitutes a minuscule, .09 percent of the U.S. workforce in a typical year.[3] Employment-based immigration is most often used to recruit highly skilled professionals to the United States; as a practical matter, it is simply not available to poor, vulnerable, and suffering persons.

USCIS also grants short-term visas in the nonimmigrant, "temporary worker" category for certain categories of jobs where people are temporarily allowed to work in the United States. Nonimmigrant, temporary visas are available in categories that include seasonal agricultural workers, nurses working in areas of professional shortage, foreign press, fashion models of distinguished merit and ability, famous athletes, artists and entertainers, exchange students, and those engaged in certain Department of Defense research. None of the people in these categories is even considered to be an "immigrant."

Nevertheless, some nonimmigrants who can demonstrate extraordinary ability in the arts, sciences education, business, or athletics, and people in certain professions and with higher education, may be eligible to get green cards and become citizens, even though they were initially granted visas as nonimmigrants. Agricultural workers, nurses, and those in low-skill jobs never have this possibility.[4]

---

3. See "USCIS Visa Availability and Priority Dates," https://www.uscis.gov/greencard/visa-availability-priority-dates; Chuck Vollmer, "2016 State of the U.S. Labor Force," Jobenomics Blog, https://jobeconomicsblog.com.

4. See USCIS, "Temporary (Non-Immigrant) Workers," https://www.uscis.

2. *Family-Based Immigration.* United States citizens and LPRs can sponsor certain close family members to become LPRs. A U.S. citizen can sponsor his or her spouse, parent (if the sponsor is over twenty-one), minor and adult children, and brothers and sisters. An LPR can sponsor a narrower group of relatives, consisting of the spouse, minor children, and adult unmarried children. In most cases, citizens and LPRs who petition for a family member must be able to prove that they earn at least 125 percent of the poverty level, and they must sign an enforceable affidavit of support for the person sponsored to that effect.[5]

Family-based immigration, sometimes called "chain migration" by its opponents, is numerically limited to 480,000 persons per year[6] and is often an exceptionally slow process. To the extent the term "chain migration" is intended to convey a never-ending, connected chain of migrants flowing into the country, it is a dishonest term. Once 480,000 family-based visas have been approved in a given year, no more are issued that year. Applicants must wait for the availability of a visa for their particular family category (for example, "adult, unmarried child of an LPR sponsor"), and for their particular home country. The waiting time differs based on three things: whether the sponsor is a citizen or an LPR, the applicant's qualifying relationship to the sponsor, and the home country. The cap on family-based visas has led to some exceptionally long waiting periods. For individuals in some categories, from some countries, USCIS is presently adjudicating applications from more than twenty years ago.

---

gov/working-united-states/temporary-nonimmigrant-workers; and USCIS, "Greencard Eligibility Categories," https://www.uscis.gov.

5. Cyrus D. Mehta, "Overview of Legal Immigration," 118, https://cyrus mehta.com/immigration-overview/

6. Immediate family members of U.S. citizens (spouses, unmarried children, and parents) are not counted in the 480,000 limit. 480,000 immigrants equaled 0.15 percent of the estimated total U.S. population in 2017 of 324,310,011, according to the U.S. Census Bureau. See Robert Schlesinger, "324 Million and Counting," *U.S. News and World Report*, December 28, 2016, https://www.usnews.com.

3. *Diversity Lottery.* The Diversity Lottery is a program of the U.S. State Department, not USCIS or the DOJ.[7] It was intended to attract a small number of immigrants from countries with historically low rates of immigration to the United States. The Diversity Lottery has its roots in an effort by Congress to help Irish immigrants in the 1980s, when thousands of Irish people had overstayed tourist visas, fleeing the political and economic "Troubles" in Ireland. A grassroots organization called the Irish Immigration Reform Movement lobbied Congress on their behalf. Congress initiated a one-time-only lottery in 1986. Of the 40,000 visas made available in that lottery, 10 percent went to Irish immigrants, even though the lottery was technically available to citizens of thirty-six countries (and Ireland was then, and is now, a country with a population smaller than New York City).[8] A second lottery occurred in 1989, widened to all but the twelve countries with the largest immigration flows to the United States.[9] In 1990, Congress made the Diversity Lottery annual and permanent in a bill that also included a three-year transitional program that legalized another 48,000 undocumented Irish immigrants.

Since 1990, the United States has made a maximum of 50,000 immigrant visas available every year, in a lottery drawn from countries with low rates of immigration to the United States.[10] These countries are no longer primarily white, European, English speaking, or Christian. From 2005 to 2014, approximately 20,000 of the winners per year were from countries in Africa.[11] Another 6,000 to 9,000 winners per year have been from Asia (defined to include Syria, United Arab Emirates, Saudi Arabia, Qatar, Oman,

---

7. See "U.S. Department of State Diversity Visa Program—Entry," https://travel.state.gov.

8. Priscilla Alvarez, "The Diversity Visa Program Was Created to Help Irish Immigrants," *The Atlantic*, November 1, 2017, https://www.theatlantic.com.

9. Alvarez, "The Diversity Visa Program."

10. See "Immigration and Nationality Act" (INA), Section 203.

11. U.S. Department of State, "Diversity Visa Program Statistics, Number of Visa Issuances and Adjustments of Status in the Diversity Immigrant Category," https://travel.state.gov.

and Yemen).[12] The only European countries with more than 1,000 winners per year were Eastern European countries: Uzbekistan, Ukraine, Turkey, Moldova, Albania, Bulgaria, Armenia, and San Marino (a micro-state within northern Italy).[13] Diversity Lottery winners these days do not fit into a white or European narrative. The Trump administration wants to end it.

The vast majority of Diversity Lottery entrants reside in their own countries until and unless they are chosen. To qualify even to enter the lottery, one must have a high school education or equivalent or, within the five years preceding the entry, have achieved at least two years of experience in an occupation requiring at least two years of training or experience.[14] Winners go through security background vetting before actually being allowed to come to the United States.

4. *Humanitarian Relief.* The final way to migrate to the United States lawfully to live and work is by obtaining some kind of humanitarian relief, including refugee or asylee status. People with refugee or asylum status are permitted to work in the United States. They may apply for citizenship after five years. The technical terms "refugee" and "asylee" do not mean what most people assume: "people fleeing really bad circumstances, seeking safety."

The United States simply does not admit most people who are legitimately fleeing persecution, terror, wars, poverty, and atrocities. Refugee and asylee status are available only to those who can prove they experienced past serious persecution in their homeland (or have a credible fear of future persecution), but only where the persecution is on account of one of the five specific grounds discussed below. Those outside the United States (not at the border) can seek protection under this same standard as refugees. People who have found their way into the United States or its border may seek asylum.[15]

---

12. Ibid.

13. Ibid.

14. Ibid.

15. This applies both to those who have entered the U.S. on a tourist visa and to those who come to the border or a port of entry and request asylum. In certain cases applicants may also request the related relief called "withholding of removal," which requires a higher showing of "clear probability of persecution."

There is a strict one-year time limit after arrival in the United States to apply for asylum (known as the "one-year bar"). Ignorance of the one-year bar does not excuse noncompliance.[16]

To qualify as either a refugee or an asylee, the burden of proof rests entirely on the applicant. It is quite high and very specific. The applicant must prove past persecution or a well-founded fear of persecution if returned to the home country, and the persecution must be because of race, religion, political opinion, national origin, or membership in a particular social group. The applicant must also prove that the government in their home country either cannot or will not protect them, and that they cannot simply relocate elsewhere in their country.[17] The legal statuses of "refugee" and "asylee" are not available to people who have been severely persecuted for other reasons, no matter how severe the persecution or compelling the story. Moreover, those suffering for reasons other than persecution, including famine, natural disaster, severe poverty, lack of medical care never qualify for asylum or refugee status, no matter how severe their suffering or how heart-wrenching their stories.

Asylum

The practice of asylum, a term meaning "what cannot be seized," originated in ancient Greece. It figures prominently in the sacred texts of Judaism, Christianity, and Islam, and imposes a duty of hospitality and protection of strangers, regardless of the cause of the persecution.[18] The first modern grant of asylum, and the origin of the term "refugee," was that of the Huguenots of southwest France. In 1685, after the revocation of the Edict of Nantes, which had offered

---

16. See Title 8 Code of Federal Regulations (8 CFR) Part 208—Procedures for Asylum and Withholding of Removal, §208.4(a)(2) One-year filing deadline, https://www.uscis.gov. In most cases, a person who enters the country seeking asylum, but who fails to file the required application within one year, will simply not be eligible for asylum, no matter his or her awareness of the one-year bar, and no matter the merits of the claim.

17. INA §208 and following.

18. Jennifer Welsh, *The Return of History: Conflict, Migration and Geopolitics in the 21st Century* (Toronto: House of Anansi Press, 2016), 115.

legal protections to those practicing Protestant religions in Catholic France, the Huguenots were faced with the choice of forced conversion to Catholicism or displacement. More than 250,000 Huguenots ultimately left France, seeking asylum in England, Wales, Scotland, Denmark, and other places. Some relocated to the English colonies in North America.[19] By the late eighteenth century, granting asylum had moved from being something the king could grant to a benefit recognized in international law as a sovereign duty of nations toward humanity, harkening back to the religious obligation to be hospitable to and to protect the stranger.[20]

The first law on asylum emerged in France, after the French Revolution, in its Constitution of 1793, which protected those who were banished from their countries "for the pursuit of liberty." Asylum became institutionalized in the world as a result of the millions of civilians displaced across Europe and Russia after World War I. In turn, World War II saw floods of refugees, including 12 million ethnic Germans who were expelled after the end of Nazi rule, 200,000 Jews fleeing renewed persecution in Eastern Europe, and more than one million other people displaced by war. The partition of India and Pakistan in 1947 and the establishment of the State of Israel in 1948 created further refugee crises.[21]

These events led to the 1950 creation of the U.N. High Commissioner for Refugees (UNHCR), a subsidiary of the U.N. General Assembly. Though originally intended to last only three years, it is today a permanent global organization. UNHCR's initial mandate was to "provide, on a non-political, humanitarian basis, international protection to refugees and to seek permanent solutions to them."[22] In July 1951, the United Nations approved its Convention relating to the Status of Refugees, which affirmed the right of persons to seek asylum from persecution in other countries, defining who can claim refugee status and setting out the rights of individu-

---

19. Ibid., 116–17.
20. Ibid., 118.
21. Ibid., 121–22.
22. Ibid., 123.

als granted asylum and the responsibilities of nations that grant asylum.[23] The UNHCR has been involved in resettling refugees in U.N. member countries following the war in Vietnam, the Balkan Wars in the 1990s, and in virtually every part of the world.[24]

The UNHCR concept of refugee/asylum was based on the principle of *non-refoulement,* a term that means people whose lives or freedom have been threatened will never be forced to return to their home countries.[25] But the U.N. standard does not actually satisfy this principle. Its definition of "refugee" and "asylee" is not nearly as broad as the religious mandate to be "hospitable to the stranger" that is at its core. Refugee means:

> Someone who has been forced to flee his or her country because of persecution, war, or violence. A refugee has *a well-founded fear of persecution for reasons of race, religion, nationality, political opinion or membership in a particular social group.*[26]

This "well-founded fear of persecution" because of one of the five factors standard is the same standard asylum seekers must meet under U.S. law. In other words, even the most severe persecution, including proven physical torture, death of family members, and the probability of death, that the applicant experiences but cannot prove to be caused by one of the five enumerated grounds will not result in a grant of refugee status or asylum.

For example, a person from Guatemala who has been persecuted by the U.S.-born gangs that systematically extort, terrorize, and murder the poor there, who has himself been physically tortured and threatened with death, and who has seen family members and neighbors killed, simply will not be granted asylum unless he can show the gang members persecuted him because of race, religion, etc. If he cannot do so, the United States will deport him or her back to Guatemala.

23. Ibid., 123.
24. Ibid., 124–27.
25. Ibid., 123.
26. USA for UNHCR, The UN Refugee Agency, "Refugee Facts," https://www.unrefugees.org/refugee-facts/what-is-a-refugee/.

While certain asylum claims are decided by USCIS (part of DHS), so-called defensive asylum claims—those raised by an undocumented person who is caught in the country and used as a defense against being deported—are determined by immigration judges in EOIR courts run by the DOJ. EOIR operates more than fifty such courthouses across the United States, each of which has multiple judges.[27]

The outcome of an asylum application depends on many factors. First, the applicant must actually know that they have to prove persecution because of one of the five factors. Many applicants do not know this when they make their way to the border, and readily admit in their initial interview by CBP that the persecution they experienced or fear was not "because of" one of the five factors. They are shocked to learn that simply proving they suffered severe persecution and that their government would not help them are not enough. The outcome of an asylum case certainly depends on the facts of the case and on the quality of the evidence and presentation (access to counsel is a significant factor in the chances of success). But the outcome also depends on factors outside the applicant's control, such as where in the United States the asylum application is made and, even within a particular courthouse, on which judge is assigned to the case.

Asylum grant rates vary wildly by judge and by location. For example, according to the Transactional Records Access Clearinghouse (TRAC), a long-term searchable study conducted and maintained by Syracuse University of asylum grant/denial rates of every U.S. immigration judge, the six-year average asylum grant rate for the eight immigration judges sitting in Arlington, Virginia (FY 2012–2017),

---

27. An applicant whose asylum claim is rejected by an immigration judge and *who has sufficient resources to do so* (which is not often the case for poor, suffering migrants escaping persecution) may appeal the judge's decision to the Board of Immigration Appeals (BIA), another office within the DOJ. If not successful before the BIA, the immigrant may then appeal to the federal appellate court in the jurisdiction. Both of these appeals must be done quickly, or they are waived. See DOJ, Board of Immigration Appeals Practice Manual, https://www.justice.gov/eoir/board-immigration-appeals-2.

was 64.9 percent (3,722 cases).[28] However, the average grant rate for the five judges sitting in Atlanta, Georgia, for the same time period was 10.2 percent (2,029 cases). In Bloomington, Indiana, one of the three assigned judges, who heard 218 cases, granted just 2.8 percent of them. The other two judges in the same location, who heard 346 and 533 cases, respectively, granted 26.6 percent and 28.9 percent. The average grant rate of the five judges in El Paso, Texas, who heard a collective 953 asylum cases during the same 2012–2017 period, was 3.3 percent. Clearly, El Paso is not a desirable place to seek asylum.

There are extensive cases and regulations that apply to every element of an asylum claim, including the procedural and substantive aspects. These include the level of proof applicants must offer to establish they have a "well-founded fear of persecution" (how likely the feared persecution has to be if the applicant is sent home), what applicants must offer to establish that they actually fit within one of the five classifications (i.e., religion, race, part of a particular social group, etc.), and what suffices to prove that the persecution an applicant fears is actually on account of the stated classification.

If an applicant claims to fear persecution because of "membership in a particular social group," the applicant must plainly identify an accepted "particular social group" and prove that his or her membership in it is due to something innate to his or her person, like gender or sexual orientation—meaning the social group cannot be "taxi drivers" or some other profession that the applicant could simply quit.[29] The particular social group cannot be too broad—like "poor people" or "children without parents." The applicant must also prove that his or her membership is immutable, socially visible, and particularly defined.[30] Consequently, the qualifying characteristic cannot be something private—it must be something about the person that is readily recognizable to the community.

28. Transactional Records Access Clearinghouse (TRAC), Syracuse University, "Judge-by-Judge Asylum Decisions in Immigration Courts FY2012–2017" (2017), https://www.trac.syr.edu/immigration/reports/judgereports/.

29. *Matter of Acosta*, 19 I&N, Dec. 211 (BIA 1985).

30. *Matter of S-E-G*, 24 I&N, Dec. 579 (BIA 2008); *Matter of E-A-G*, 24 I&N, Dec. 591 (BIA 2008).

Applicants may prove a well-founded fear of persecution based on proof of actual past persecution, but the government can defeat such a claim by establishing that conditions in the home country or town have changed. Applicants must prove that their own governments cannot or will not protect them, and that they cannot relocate to safety within their own countries.[31] These are but a few of the many elements of an asylum case. Ignoring the extensive case law (precedent) that exists on every element can be a quick road to denial of asylum. Thus, an applicant, even with the most meritorious claim, who lacks documentary proof and access to experienced counsel is unlikely to succeed.[32]

The United States accepts only a fraction of the world's refugees—specifically persons located outside the United States and who have been determined to meet the refugee standard. According to the Pew Research Center, in the thirty-seven years since the passage of the Refugee Act of 1980, the United States has accepted about three million refugees. From 1990 to 1995, the United States accepted an average of 112,000 refugees per year. In 2002, following the terrorist attacks of 2001, the number dropped to 27,000. Today, refugee applicants tend not to be primarily white Christians. The fiscal year of 2016, the year prior to the Trump administration, reveals the following statistics: of the 84,995 refugees admitted, 46 percent (39,000) were Muslim (the highest percentage ever), and approximately 29 percent were from African countries such as the Democratic Republic of Congo and Somalia.[33]

---

31. See *Secaida-Rosales v. INS*, 331 F. 3d 297, 306 (2d Cir. 2003); 8 C.F.R. §208.13(b)(1)(i)(A) and (B).

32. For this reason, asylum grant rates of judges seated at Adelanto Detention Center, a remote private immigration prison in San Bernardino County, California, in an area where few lawyers practice, are low—in the 10 percent range. TRAC, Syracuse University, "Judge-by-Judge Asylum Decisions, FY2012–2017" (2017).

33. Jens Manuel Krogstad and Jynnah Radford, "Key Facts about Refugees to the U.S.," Pew Research Center Fact Tank, News in the Numbers, January 30, 2017, https://www.pewresearch.org.

In the United States, the president decides how many refugees will be admitted to the country each year. In September 2017, Mr. Trump announced that the United States would reduce the number of refugees accepted in the fiscal year that commenced October 1, 2017, to a maximum of 45,000.[34] This was the lowest number of refugees the country had agreed to accept in the seventy-year world history of refugee resettlement.

In announcing the subsequent U.S. withdrawal from the U.N. Global Compact on Migration in December 2017, Mr. Trump's ambassador to the United Nations, Nikki Haley, baldly stated that a global approach to the world's refugee crisis is "simply not compatible with U.S. sovereignty."[35] In 2019, the administration reduced the maximum number of refugees to 18,000 for fiscal year 2020. It is beyond dispute that asylum and refugee status are extraordinarily difficult to obtain and, in any event, apply only to a small fraction of the suffering people in the world.[36]

Other Forms of Relief for Noncitizens

In addition to the four legal roads to immigrate to the United States, there are several additional forms of relief that can be raised by a person in the country without documents—either a person who has not been caught or a person in removal proceedings—as a defense to being deported.[37] They can also be raised by immigrants already

---

34. Dara Lind, "The Trump Administration Doesn't Believe in the Global Refugee Crisis," *Vox*, December 4, 2017, https://www.vox.com. In comparison, in the previous two fiscal years, the Obama administration set its refugee ceiling to "at least 100,000."

35. Lind, "The Trump Administration Doesn't Believe."

36. During Fiscal Year 2016, 65,218 people sought asylum in the United States. Of these people, 52,109 asylum cases were completed, and 43 percent were granted (24,435 people). Of the asylum grants, 35.56 percent were persons from China. Executive Office for Immigration Review FY 2016 Statistics Yearbook, Office of Planning, Analysis, and Statistics (March 2017), pp. K1, L1, https://www.justice.gov/eoir/page/file/fysb16/download.

37. On June 28, 2018, the Trump administration announced that going forward, if an undocumented person seeks one of these benefits from USCIS and is

in the United States without legal status who are victims of certain kinds of child abuse, domestic violence, human trafficking, sexual assault, and related harms.

The procedure to obtain each form of relief is different, quite challenging, and, as with asylum, the burden of proving eligibility rests squarely on the applicant. Applicants may be represented by lawyers, but they are not entitled to a lawyer at government expense. The forms of relief are (1) Special Immigrant Juvenile Status; (2) U nonimmigrant status (U visa); (3) T nonimmigrant status (T visa); (4) the Violence Against Women Act (VAWA) self-petition; (5) VAWA cancellation; and (6) waivers for battered children and spouses.[38]

1. *Special Immigrant Juvenile Status* (SIJS). SIJS was created by Congress in the Immigration Act of 1990, which amended the Immigration and Nationality Act of 1965. An immigrant who is present in the United States, under twenty-one years of age, and unmarried may apply to USCIS for a determination of SIJS and, if granted, may apply to be an LPR, if and when a visa is available for his/her country and category, as discussed above. But as Gabriela's, Javi's, and Liliana's stories demonstrate, Congress decided that in order for a child to apply to USCIS for SIJS, the child must possess an order from a state court judge making factual findings that

    (a) the child is either in the custody of the state (i.e., foster care or a state facility) or has been placed (by the state) in the custody of an adult;

    (b) the child was "abused, abandoned or neglected" by one or both parents in the child's home country;

    (c) reunification with that parent is not "viable"; and

---

unsuccessful, the person will be referred to EOIR immigration court for removal proceedings. This policy serves to discourage undocumented people (who have not been caught) from applying for benefits to which they may be entitled, for fear they will be deported, https://www.uscis.gov.

38. Poojna Asnani and Deborah Lee, "Representing Vulnerable Immigrants (Dec. 2015)," P.L.I, *Defending Immigration Removal Proceedings, 2017* (New York: Practicing Law Institute, 2017), 141–93.

(d) it is not in the child's best interest to be returned to the home country.[39]

Congress dictated that these findings can be made only by a state court judge—neither USCIS nor EOIR immigration judges are allowed to make them, nor to look behind and second-guess the findings of the state court judge.[40]

In practice, this means that children who were abandoned, abused, or neglected in their home countries, who have come to the United States seeking help, and who have been placed in removal proceedings before an immigration judge have the opportunity to file a completely separate lawsuit in a state court—at their own expense—seeking to persuade a local judge to make the required eligibility findings so that the child can then apply to USCIS (not the immigration judge) for SIJS. If the child obtains SIJS findings from a state court judge, she or he can send those findings to USCIS with an application for special immigrant juvenile status, a nineteen-page form, and, if granted, can apply separately to the immigration judge to close the removal case.

In the separate state court case, the child has the burden of proof under the laws of whatever state in which she or he happens to be located. In other words, the child must follow local law and produce actual evidence to persuade the judge that he or she was "abused, abandoned or neglected" by at least one parent in the home country,

---

39. INA § 101(a)(27)(J) (definition of SIJS); INA § 245(h) (adjustment of status and inadmissibility for special immigrant juveniles); 8 U.S.C. § 1232 (William Wilberforce Trafficking Victims Protection Reauthorization Act of 2008; "TVPRA"); 8 C.F.R. § 204.11(a) (definition), § 204.11(b) (SIJS filings), § 204.11(c)(SIJS eligibility), § 204.11(d) (documents filed), and § 245.1(e)(2)(vi) (B)(3) (inadmissibility).

40. See 8 U.S.C. §1101(a)(27)(J) and 8 C.F.R. §204.11(c). Notwithstanding this statutory prohibition, and contrary to federal law, since the beginning of the Trump administration, USCIS has regularly been demanding that SIJS applicants provide documentary evidence for USCIS to review to evaluate state court judges' SIJS findings. Furthermore, USCIS regularly disregards the 180-day statutory time limit for adjudication of SIJS applications under §235(d)(2) of the TVPRA, sometimes taking more than a year.

that it is not "viable" to reunite with the abusive parent, and that it is in the child's best interest to remain in the United States. Evidence to support these findings might include the child's own testimony, testimony of relatives, photographs, birth certificate, medical records, school records (from both the home country and the United States), and the like. Documents in languages other than English typically must be translated and certified before being submitted to court. Most state court systems require that the child prove that, if the child cannot procure that parent's consent, all the papers filed in court in the United States were legally "served" on the abusive or neglectful parent(s) in the home country.

2. *U Nonimmigrant Status.* Noncitizens present in the United States who are crime victims may apply for this status if they are

(a) victims of qualifying and serious criminal activity that occurred within the United States;
(b) have suffered substantial harm as a result of the criminal activity;
(c) possess information about that criminal activity; and
(d) cooperate with the investigation or prosecution of that criminal activity.[41] This status is not available to victims of crime outside the United States or on the way here.

U status can be sought only through a detailed, written application directly to USCIS. Immigration judges cannot approve such visas. The U applicant must provide evidence of the crime and that she or he suffered "substantial harm" as a result of it. This might include medical/psychiatric records, police reports, and written witness accounts. Not all harm constitutes "substantial" harm. The applicant for this kind of relief must also present a "certifi-

---

41. See INA §§101, 212, 214, 245 and 8 C.F.R. §§103, 212, 214, 245, and 274a. Under INA §101(a)(15)(U)(iii), a U petition may be based on being a victim (not a witness or bystander) of enumerated serious crimes, such as abduction, sexual abuse, blackmail, female genital mutilation, incest, involuntary servitude, manslaughter, murder, stalking, torture, trafficking, and the like. Many seemingly serious crimes do not qualify.

cation" from a specified federal, state, or local law enforcement official that confirms that the U applicant helpfully cooperated with either the investigation or the prosecution of the crime. There are no exceptions to this requirement.[42] Otherwise successful U applicants are still subject to virtually all grounds of inadmissibility under INA §212(a), such as those excluding persons with communicable diseases, mental disorders, drug abuse history, criminal records, and the like, although applicants may apply for waivers of some grounds.

U applicants may petition for certain derivative family members to be allowed to stay in the United States with them.[43] Successful applicants (and their derivative family members) are authorized to work in the United States and may eventually apply to become LPRs if they can show that their continued presence in the United States is justified on humanitarian grounds or is otherwise in the public interest, among other requirements.[44] Like children who petition for SIJS, U applicants are often in removal proceedings in immigration court when they pursue U status. U applicants may ask the court to postpone their cases while they pursue U status with USCIS. In fiscal year 2016, USCIS received 35,000 U applications; 10,000 of them—the annual cap—were approved. A backlog of 86,980 applications remained pending.[45]

3. *T Nonimmigrant Status.* Noncitizen victims of a "severe form of trafficking," who are present in the United States as a result of the trafficking, who have complied with reasonable requests for assistance in the investigation or prosecution of trafficking (unless

---

42. If the U applicant is under sixteen years of age at the time of the crime or is otherwise incapacitated, a guardian or other adult may provide the information and cooperation, and obtain the certification—for the child.

43. See INA §101(a)(15)(U)(ii)(I) (applicants twenty years of age and younger may sponsor parents and unmarried siblings); INA §101(a)(15)(U)(ii)(II) (applicants twenty-one years of age and older may sponsor only spouses and children), and C.F.R. §212(14)(f).

44. See INA §245 and 8 C.F.R. §245.24.

45. USCIS, "Number of Form 918, Petition for U Nonimmigrant Status by Fiscal Year, Quarter and Case Status, 2009–2017," https://www.uscis.gov.

the victim is seventeen or younger), and who would suffer "extreme hardship involving unusual and severe harm" if returned home, may be eligible for T nonimmigrant status.[46] "Severe" trafficking means either sex trafficking, in which a commercial sex act is induced by force, fraud, or coercion and the victim is under eighteen, or labor trafficking, in which a person is recruited, transported, harbored for labor or services by force, fraud, coercion, or is subjected to involuntary servitude or slavery.[47] The law also defines the terms "coercion" and "serious harm" with specificity. Applicants may establish that they are victims of a "severe form of trafficking" by submitting (with their application) an endorsement (on a specific federal form) from a law enforcement agency or by presenting credible "secondary evidence" (meaning trial transcripts, police reports, news articles, and the like) proving the nature and scope of the force, fraud, or coercion used against them. Thus, in contrast to the U status, law enforcement certification is not required, but applicants may offer it. Applicants may also submit their own affidavits and testimony from other witnesses to support their applications.[48]

A T-status applicant may not argue that leaving the United States would cause "extreme hardship involving unusual and severe harm," based on alleged current or future economic detriment, or lack of social or economic opportunities outside the United States.[49] The extreme hardship standard could, however, be met by proving serious physical or mental illness as a result of the trafficking that necessitates treatment not available elsewhere, the likelihood of retaliation against the victim if returned, the likelihood of revictimization outside the United States, and other such factors. The critical point, here, is that the applicant must prove this factor with actual evidence, not merely assert it.

---

46. See INA §§101(a)(15)(T), 214(o), 212(d)(13), 245(l) and 8 C.F.R. §§103(7) (b–c), 212.16, 212.18, 214.11, 247a.12(a)(16), 247a.12(c)(25), and 245.23.

47. See INA §101(a)(15)(T)(i)(I); §103 of the TVPRA; and Division A of the Victims of Trafficking and Violence Protection Act of 2000, Pub. l. 106–386.

48. See 8 C.F.R. §214.11(f)(3).

49. See 8 C.F.R. §214.11(i)(1).

USCIS has exclusive jurisdiction over adjudication of T status, with a cap of only five thousand grants per year. Immigration judges cannot approve T status. If granted, T status generally lasts for four years. Certain close family members may be granted derivative status. A recipient may typically apply to become an LPR after three years.

4. *Violence Against Women (VAWA) Self-Petitions.* Created in 1994, the "VAWA self-petition" refers to a cluster of statutory provisions under INA §204(a)(1) that allows people with qualifying close family relationships to an abusive U.S. citizen or LPR to petition for family-based immigration status, without having to rely on the abusive family member to petition for them—hence the "self-petition" characterization.[50] Successful VAWA self-petitioners whose qualifying family member is a citizen are immediately eligible to apply for LPR status.[51] Successful VAWA self-petitioners whose qualifying family member is an LPR must wait for a visa to become available for their country and in their category, like those whose LPR family member petitioned for them.[52] Approved VAWA self-petitioners are eligible for work permits. Their children may receive derivative status simultaneously if they are present in the United States. VAWA self-petitioners receive deferred action in removal proceedings (in court), while they wait to apply for LPR status.[53]

VAWA self-petitions are exclusively decided by USCIS. To be eligible, the self-petitioner must prove (with evidence) a qualifying family relationship: marriage (either current or which ended in the past two years) or parent–child (the self-petitioner may be either the child or the parent of an abusive adult).[54] The VAWA self-petitioner must prove that she or he jointly resided with the abuser and that he or she suffered "battery or extreme cruelty" at the hands of the

---

50. Asnani and Lee, "Representing Vulnerable Immigrants," 141–94, 173.
51. Ibid. See also INA §§245(a) and (c).
52. Asnani and Lee, "Representing Vulnerable Immigrants."
53. Ibid.
54. Ibid. See also INA §204.

abuser.[55] VAWA self-petitioners must also prove that they are of good moral character.[56]

The requirement that the VAWA self-petitioner must be a victim of abuse by a U.S. citizen or LPR spouse or parent/child with whom the petitioner jointly resided means that the relief is practically available only to a narrow category of people who themselves have lived in the United States for a significant period of time and who suffered very serious abuse at the hands of the qualifying family member that they are willing to report to law enforcement. While it can be important as a defense to removal for some people, VAWA self-petition simply does not offer a road to lawful status for new or recent immigrants or to those whose abusers are undocumented.

5. *VAWA Cancellation.* VAWA cancellation is the popular term for "Cancellation of Removal and Adjustment of Status for Certain Nonpermanent Residents, Special Rule for Battered Spouse or Child." It is an entirely different category than VAWA self-petition. VAWA cancellation allows noncitizens who are in removal proceedings, who are victims of domestic violence perpetrated on them by a qualifying U.S. citizen or LPR relative, to obtain cancellation of their removal from the country.[57] The remedy is available only to persons who have been present in the United States for at least three years and are inadmissible or deportable but who also can demonstrate they suffered battery or extreme cruelty at the hands of their qualifying family-member abuser.

VAWA cancellation can be ordered only by an immigration judge—USCIS has no jurisdiction to consider these applications. A successful application results in automatic LPR status, permission to work, and the right to apply for citizenship in five years. But VAWA cancellation is extremely limited—only four thousand applications may be granted per year, and each grant anywhere in the country counts toward the cap. While it may be an extremely helpful defense for victims of severe abuse who have lived in the United States for

55. Asnani and Lee, "Representing Vulnerable Immigrants."
56. Ibid.
57. See INA §240A.

some years, VAWA cancellation is not a remedy available to more recent immigrants, those seeking to enter the United States, or people abused by undocumented persons.[58]

6. *Battered Spouse and Child Waivers.* This quite limited category applies only to persons who have already obtained conditional permanent resident status under INA §216 through the sponsorship of a qualified family member (see Family-Based Immigration on p. 156). The process allows these people to request that conditions to their ongoing lawful permanent residency be removed, without the support of the formerly sponsoring family member, because the petitioner "was battered by or was the subject of extreme cruelty perpetrated by" that person. This remedy is obviously quite important for vulnerable family members who have been severely abused by their family sponsor, but it does not provide independent relief for newcomers to the country.

DACA and TPS

There are two additional groups of noncitizens who—as of this writing—possess limited authorization to reside and work in the United States temporarily. Both of these groups have received significant press attention. Each group has a vocal group of supporters. The first group are recipients of "deferred action" (the "action" in question is being deported from the country) through the Deferred Action for Childhood Arrivals program (DACA). This program was created by President Obama in 2012, without congressional approval. Under DACA, the deportation of a qualified person, who was brought to the United States without permission before they turned sixteen,

---

58. In 2018, then attorney general Jeff Sessions imposed quotas on the EOIR immigration judges, requiring that they avoid postponements in cases on their dockets and instead must close at least seven hundred cases per year to remain in good standing. EOIR judges are employees of the Department of Justice, reporting to the attorney general. That same year, in a case called *Matter of Castro-Tum*, Sessions also directed that immigration judges could no longer "administratively close" cases on their dockets while the respondent sought relief with USCIS. On August 29, 2019, the U.S. Court of Appeals for the Fourth Circuit overturned Sessions's direction to end the judges' ability to "administratively close" cases.

was continuously present in the United States since June 15, 2007, was at least fifteen years old when they applied for DACA, paid a fee (almost $500), and provided biometric and residential information to USCIS, could be deferred for two years, subject to potential (but not guaranteed) renewal. DACA recipients were eligible to apply for similarly time-limited but renewable work permits.

Most important, the DACA program never included any path for recipients to remain in the United States permanently, to become LPRs or citizens. It was conceived by Mr. Obama as a temporary reprieve from deportation, coupled with a temporary work permit, in exchange for a fee and information, including biometrics where the applicant lived.

Created without congressional approval, DACA was rescinded by President Trump on September 5, 2017, without congressional approval. The announcement allowed a brief period for those whose DACA was about to expire to seek one last renewal period. As of 2019, approximately 700,000 young people were enrolled in the DACA program.[59] Mr. Trump's rescission of the DACA program was promptly challenged in the courts on the basis that the rescission announcement lacked coherent reasoning. The courts enjoined the termination of DACA, and USCIS has been ordered to continue to accept DACA renewal applications while the court process continues. No new DACA applications have been accepted. The challenge to the termination of DACA was heard by the U.S. Supreme Court in 2019. The decision is expected in 2020. But even if the Supreme Court were to uphold the injunction, the Trump administration could remedy the basis for it (the alleged failure to provide coherent reasoning) by providing a new, more fulsome explanation for the rescission. Thus, the long-term viability of DACA is doubtful.

The second group authorized to live and work in the United States (but not stay permanently) are those with "temporary protected

---

59. Lori Robertson, "The DACA Population Numbers," FactCheck.Org, https://www.factcheck.org. USCIS itself has stated that as of September 4, 2017, the day before Mr. Trump terminated the program, there were 689,800 active DACA recipients.

status" (TPS). Congress created the TPS program in 1990. Under this program, the secretary of DHS has discretion to designate (and de-designate) foreign countries for TPS for short periods of time (six to eighteen months) due to conditions in those countries that temporarily prevent the country's nationals in the United States from returning home safely or, in certain circumstances, when the country is unable to handle the return of its own people.[60] Citizens of TPS-designated countries who apply and provide biometric and residential information to USCIS can receive work permits during their stays in the United States.

As of July 2019, ten countries remained designated for TPS. Most of these countries had their brief TPS designations extended repeatedly under prior presidential administrations. For example, El Salvador was first designated for TPS under President George W. Bush, following a series of earthquakes there in 2001 that displaced 17 percent of El Salvador's population. Since then, TPS for El Salvador has been extended throughout presidential administrations. Haiti was designated for TPS based on a 2010 earthquake and has also been extended repeatedly since then.

In its first thirteen months, the Trump administration announced the termination of the TPS designations for El Salvador, Haiti, Sudan, and Nicaragua. Beneficiaries immediately challenged these terminations in federal courts. The courts enjoined the terminations, and, as with DACA, beneficiaries are allowed to remain in the country while the court challenges go forward. In late October 2019, the Trump administration announced that like its predecessors, it would extend TPS for the approximately 200,000 El Salvadorians living in the United States for another short period— through January 4, 2021. This move reversed the administration's previous termination of TPS for persons from El Salvador.[61]

All TPS beneficiaries have provided their biometrics and residential addresses to USCIS. They are subject to being forcibly removed

---

60. See USCIS, "Temporary Protected Status," https://www.uscis.gov.

61. Richard Gonzales, "Administration Extends Temporary Protected Status to Many Salvadorans in U.S.," NPR, October 28, 2019, https//www.npr.org.

from the country if they do not voluntarily depart when their TPS designation ends (subject, of course, to the court challenges). As of 2017, there were an estimated 325,000 people from TPS countries residing in the United States.[62] About 68,000 TPS beneficiaries (22 percent) arrived in the United States as children.[63] Approximately 270,000 U.S.-born children (American citizens) have parents who are TPS beneficiaries from El Salvador, Haiti, and Honduras.[64] TPS has never included a path to living in the United States permanently, becoming an LPR, or obtaining citizenship.

---

62. Robert Warren and Donald Kerwin, Center for Migration Studies, "A Statistical and Demographic Profile of the U.S. Temporary Protected Status Populations from El Salvador, Honduras and Haiti," *Journal of Migration and Human Security* 5, no. 3 (2017): 557–92.

63. Warren and Kerwin, "A Statistical and Demographic Profile."

64. CAP Immigration Team, "TPS Holders in the United States," Center for American Progress, https://cdn.americanprogress.org.

Glossary

Apostolic constitution is a form of papal decree dealing with matters of faith of the universal Roman Catholic Church. It is the most solemn form of legislation issued by the pope to the universal church.

Asylee is the legal term for a person who has received asylum.

Asylum is a form of protection available to persons who meet the legal definition of "refugee" but who are at the U.S. border or already in the country. To qualify for asylum, a person must prove they have suffered severe persecution or reasonably fear they will suffer severe persecution in their home country because of their race, religion, nationality, political opinion, or membership in a particular social group.

Cartels are vicious criminal organizations that wreak havoc in Central and South America, as they bring illicit drugs to the American consumer. Since the 1980s, cartels have grown, splintered, forged alliances, broken alliances, and gone to war with one another over territory and trade routes. The Mexican cartels presently include the Sinaloa Cartel, the Jalisco New Generation, the Juarez Cartel, the Gulf Cartel, Los Zetas, and the Beltran-Leyva Organization. New leaders and new groups are constantly emerging. The cartels' combined income is estimated to be tens of billions of dollars a year, largely fueled by the American appetite for illicit drugs.

Common good is the Catholic concept that stems from natural law's recognition that humans are social creatures and that our human need to live in society with other people is intrinsic to our God-given human nature. Living in societies necessitates that we have human laws—laws that are created by humans (not God) in specific times and situations—for the common good of all the people. Human laws for the common good refer to laws that form a social order that enable all the people in the world (not some or even most of them) to find their way to God.

Customs and Border Protection (CBP), which replaced the old "Border Patrol" after the terrorist attacks of 2001, is a federal agency that is part of DHS. CBP is responsible for protecting the border—including inspections, expedited removals (immediate deportation upon apprehension, without further due process), and border surveillance.

Declaration is written testimony in the witness's own words, under penalty of perjury.

Deferred Action for Childhood Arrivals (DACA) is a program created by executive order of President Obama in 2012, without congressional approval. Under DACA, the deportation of a qualified person, who was brought to the United States without permission before they turned sixteen, was continuously present in the United States since June 15, 2007, was at least fifteen years old when they applied for DACA, paid a fee (almost $500), and provided biometric and residential information to USCIS, could be deferred for two years, subject to potential (but not guaranteed) renewal. DACA recipients were eligible to apply for similarly time-limited but renewable work permits. DACA was rescinded by President Trump in September 2017. The rescission was enjoined by the courts; DACA recipients have been able to renew their participation in the program while the court case progressed, but no new DACA applications have been accepted. The U.S. Supreme Court will announce its decision on DACA in 2020.

Deferred Action for Parents of Americans (DAPA) was an immigration policy announced by executive order of President Obama in November 2014, under which certain undocumented persons who had lived in the United States since 2010 and were the parents of either American citizens or green card holders (LPRs) could apply to have their deportation deferred for a specific period of time and receive a work permit. In February 2015, at the request of twenty-six states, a district court judge in Texas enjoined DAPA from going into effect. The federal Fifth Circuit Court of Appeals upheld the injunction, and in June 2016, the then eight-member U.S. Supreme Court deadlocked 4-4, thereby leaving the injunction in place. DAPA never went into effect.

Department of Health and Human Services (HHS) is a cabinet-level department of the federal government with the mission of protecting the health of Americans and providing essential human services. HHS is administered by the secretary of human services, appointed by the president and confirmed by the Senate. In the area of immigration, HHS is responsible for the Office of Refugee Resettlement, which is part of HHS's Administration for Children and Families.

Department of Homeland Security (DHS) is a cabinet-level department of the U.S. federal government, created after the terrorist attacks of September 11, 2001, responsible for public security. Its missions involve antiterrorism, border security, immigration, customs, cyber security, and disaster prevention. DHS is led by the secretary of homeland security, appointed by the president and confirmed by the Senate. In terms of immigration, USCIS, ICE, and CBP are agencies subordinate to DHS.

Department of Justice (DOJ) is a cabinet-level department of the U.S. federal government, responsible for the enforcement of law and administration of justice in the country. The DOJ is headed by the U.S. attorney general, who is nominated by the president and confirmed by the Senate. EOIR, the immigration court system, is subordinate to DOJ.

Department of State (DOS) is a cabinet-level department of the federal government with the mission of carrying out foreign policy and international relations. DOS is headed by the secretary of state, who is nominated by the president and confirmed by the Senate. DOS and its **Bureau of Consular Affairs (BCA)** are responsible for the Diversity Lottery, admissibility to the country (from foreign consulates), the consular "lookout and support system" for national security, and for determining refugee priorities.

Diversity Lottery is a U.S. government program started in the 1980s that eventually became part of the Immigration and Nationality Act, passed by Congress, under which a small number of healthy, educated, and noncriminal, employable people (fifty thousand persons per year) are selected by lottery to migrate to the United States from countries with low representation.

18th Street gang, also known as Mara 18, Barrio 18, and La 18, is a vicious criminal gang that, like its principal rival, Mara Salvatrucha, started as a street gang in Los Angeles in the 1970s and 1980s. As refugees from wars in Central America, young men organized to defend themselves from existing gangs in Los Angeles. The 18th Street gang started near 18th St. and Union Avenue in the Rampart section of Los Angeles. In the 1990s, 18th Street gang members were deported from the United States back to Central America. The gang is now responsible for extreme violence and criminal activity in El Salvador, Honduras, Guatemala, Mexico, and many other countries.

Employment-based migration is one of the four roads to legal migration to the United States. It is available (on other than a nonimmigrant, temporary basis) only to professionals and other highly skilled persons through a corporate sponsor who can prove that no one already in the country can do the job. Employment-based migration is limited to 140,000 persons per year.

Encyclical is a papal letter to all the bishops of the Catholic Church on matters of doctrine, morals, or discipline, meant to be spread throughout the church community.

Executive Office of Immigration Review (EOIR) is the federal administrative court system for immigration. EOIR is part of the DOJ, not DHS. EOIR judges decide outcomes for people—both detained and nondetained—who are in removal proceedings, including asylum claims and appeals.

Family-based migration, sometimes derogatorily called "chain migration," is one of the four roads to legal migration to the United States. Citizens and green card holders may sponsor a relative to migrate to the United States. Only 480,000 people per year are allowed to migrate on this basis. Waiting times for family-based visas can exceed twenty years.

Guardian *ad litem* refers to a noncustodial guardian appointed to advise the court from the perspective of the best interest of the child. Family courts in California will not hear a case involving children and their parents without a guardian *ad litem*.

Guatemalan National Civil Police (PNC), the supposedly "reformed" national police of Guatemala, re-created after the conclusion of the 1996 Guatemalan civil war, is considered today to be among the most corrupt and criminal police forces in the Western Hemisphere.

Humanitarian migration refers to various forms of immigration relief, including asylum and refugee status, and is available to people based on their having suffered serious persecution in their own countries or having suffered as victims of serious crimes perpetrated by U.S. citizens or green card holders. The term "humanitarian migration" is broad; but the specific categories that fall within the term are extremely narrow, and the requirements to qualify are strictly interpreted.

Immigration and Customs Enforcement (ICE) is an agency created after September 11, 2001, that is part of DHS. ICE is responsible for the enforcement of the law within the country, including apprehension of undocumented persons, workplace raids, detention, processing, and deportations.

Immigration and Naturalization Service (INS) was the federal agency responsible for immigration, which was dissolved when DHS was created after the terrorist events of September 11, 2001.

International Commission against Impunity in Guatemala (CICIG) was a U.N.-backed group whose purpose was to provide external assistance to Guatemalan prosecutors and police in rooting out and prosecuting corruption within government structures.

Lawful permanent resident (LPR) is the formal term for a green card holder, a noncitizen who has been granted authorization to live and work in the United States indefinitely.

Mara Salvatrucha, also known as MS-13, is a criminal gang that originated in Los Angeles, California, in the 1970s and 1980s, as Central Americans who had immigrated to the United States during decades of civil wars organized to protect themselves from existing gangs in the Los Angeles area. Over time, Mara Salvatrucha grew in both organization and viciousness. MS-13 members were deported to Central America in the late 1990s, taking the gang with them. MS-13 now operates with relative impunity in many parts of Central America.

Moral absolutes are, in the Catholic tradition, exceptionless moral norms ("acts which per se and in themselves, independent of circumstances, are always seriously wrong by reason of their object").

Natural law refers to the part of God's eternal law that concerns humans on earth—God's way for us or, in other words, God's universal principles for how God's world works best and how we must act in it. Since the thirteenth century, Thomas Aquinas has been generally seen as the master systematician of a natural law that is based on the creator God—who created us in God's own image—and God's divine providence. Aquinas's description of natural law, and his deep wrestling with all of its implications, underlies Catholic respect for life, including the teachings about what human life *is* and is *for*.

Non-Immigrant Visa is a form of limited permission to enter the United States and work for brief, specified time periods. Recipients are required to leave the country at the end of that period.

Office of Refugee Resettlement (ORR) is responsible for assisting refugees to acclimate to new lives in the United States. Since 2003, ORR has also been responsible for the care and placement of unaccompanied children apprehended by agencies of DHS, including ICE and CBP.

Pro bono lawyer is a one who works on a case without charging a fee, "for the public good."

Proof texting is the practice of picking through the Bible to find quotations that—in isolation and out of context—might seem to support a proposition.

Refugee is a status awarded by the U.N. High Commission for Refugees (UNHCR) to certain persons who have fled their countries because of persecution, war, or violence, and who can demonstrate a well-founded fear of persecution if returned, because of race, religion, nationality, political opinion, or membership in a particular social group. Since the conclusion of World War II, the United

States has accepted hundreds of thousands of persons whom the UNHCR has determined to be refugees under this standard from around the world. In 2019, after initially indicating that the United States would no longer accept any refugees at all, President Trump reduced the number of refugees to be accepted in the United States during the next fiscal year to 18,000.

Special Immigrant Juvenile Status (SIJS) is a legal status created by Congress in 1990, when it amended the Immigration and Nationality Act of 1965. Under this longstanding U.S. law, children who have come to the United States under the age of twenty-one (and who are unmarried) and who have been placed under the jurisdiction of a state court or its designee may apply to USCIS for SIJS if they can present an order from a state court judge determining that they were abandoned, abused, or neglected by one or both parents in their home country, that reunification with that parent is not viable, and that being returned to their home country is not in their best interest. Recipients of SIJS may apply for green cards and become citizens.

Temporary Protected Status (TPS) is a program created by Congress in 1990 to provide brief periods of assistance to people in crisis from other countries. Congress authorized the federal government to give brief respites (six to eighteen months) in this country to people whose homelands had suffered sudden emergency situations that left them temporarily unable to safeguard their citizens. Beneficiaries of TPS are told from inception that they are not immigrants and that they can stay and work in the country only for the short term. Successive presidential administrations have extended TPS for many countries.

Unaccompanied child. In U.S. immigration law, unaccompanied children are foreign born, noncitizen minors who arrive in the country unaccompanied by a parent or legal guardian.

United States Citizenship and Immigration Services (USCIS) is an agency created by Congress in 2003 in the wake of the 2001 terrorist attacks and falls under the Department of Homeland Security (DHS). Among other things, USCIS is involved in the selection of immigrants for various benefits, eligibility for asylum (for some immigrants), work permits, and naturalization.

Utilitarianism is a group of nineteenth-century consequentialist ethical theories associated with Jeremy Bentham and John Stuart Mill, aimed at maximizing "utility" by seeking the "greatest good for the greatest number." Utilitarian theories embrace the notion that it is legitimate to pursue an outcome or social policy under which some people lose out entirely, but *more* people thrive.

Index